A CRY OF ABSENCE

A CRY OF ABSENCE

---

*The True Story of a Father's Search
for His Kidnapped Children*

ANDREW WARD, 1946-

VIKING

VIKING
Published by the Penguin Group
Viking Penguin Inc., 40 West 23rd Street,
New York, New York 10010, U.S.A.
Penguin Books Ltd, 27 Wrights Lane,
London W8 5TZ, England
Penguin Books Australia Ltd, Ringwood,
Victoria, Australia
Penguin Books Canada Ltd, 2801 John Street,
Markham, Ontario, Canada L3R 1B4
Penguin Books (N.Z.) Ltd, 182–190 Wairau Road,
Auckland 10, New Zealand

Penguin Books Ltd, Registered Offices:
Harmondsworth, Middlesex, England

First published in 1988 by Viking Penguin Inc.
Published simultaneously in Canada

1 3 5 7 9 10 8 6 4 2

Grateful acknowledgment is made for permission to reprint an excerpt
from "Winter Remembered" from *Selected Poems*, Third Edition, Re-
vised and Enlarged by John Crowe Ransom. Copyright 1924 by Alfred
A. Knopf, Inc.; renewed 1952 by John Crowe Ransom. By permission
of Alfred A.Knopf, Inc.

LIBRARY OF CONGRESS CATALOGING IN PUBLICATION DATA
Ward, Andrew, 1946–
A cry of absence.
Bibliography: p.
1. Kidnapping, Parental—United States—Case studies.
2. Kidnapping, Parental—Israel—Case studies.
I. Title.
HV6598.W37 1988   364.1'54   87-40459
ISBN 0-670-82217-5

Printed in the United States of America by
Arcata Graphics, Fairfield, Pennsylvania
Set in Sabon

For Ben, Sara, and Mag

Two evils, monstrous either one apart,
Possessed me, and were long and loath at going:
A cry of Absence, Absence in the heart,
And in the wood the furious winter blowing.

JOHN CROWE RANSOM
Winter Remembered

CONTENTS

AUTHOR'S NOTE   *xi*

1 THE CAST   *1*

2 BARBARA   *11*

3 THE CONVERSION   *19*

4 THE CHICKEN HOUSE   *30*

5 THE LIFE RAFT   *39*

6 SUSAN   *50*

7 THE COINS   *59*

8 THE VISITATION   *68*

9 25 BRISBY STREET   *78*

10 *HABEAS CORPUS*   *92*

11 ON THE CASE   *101*

12 NOT SO FAST   *108*

13 UFAP   *116*

14 THE LETTER   *127*

15 THE WAKE   *135*

16 SID   *145*

17 ABRAMSON   *156*

18 PASSPORTS   165

19 BEST-LAID PLANS   172

20 VISAS   182

21 NO PLACE FOR CHILDREN   188

22 THE CROSSING   197

23 GRACE   205

    EPILOGUE   210

    NOTES   213

    ACKNOWLEDGMENTS   217

    SOURCES   219

AUTHOR'S NOTE

The following is Thomas Osborne's own story of his search for his kidnapped children. All of the names, identities, and locations within the United States and Israel, including those of Thomas Osborne and his family, have been disguised to protect his children. I am indebted to the real Thomas Osborne and his family, as well as many of the participants in his search, for so generously and painstakingly sharing his story with me.

A CRY OF ABSENCE

1

THE CAST

On the eve of my eleventh birthday in 1956, I was pausing by the curb on my bicycle when an elderly woman named Folkes mistook her accelerator for her brake and came roaring down the street. By the time her gray Plymouth hit me, she must have been going forty miles an hour: fast enough, at any rate, to hurl me twenty feet before finally coming to rest on my leg.

My cries roused the neighborhood. Confused, I suppose, by the children screaming and the neighbors rushing out in their slippers and shirtsleeves, Mrs. Folkes threw her car into reverse and backed over me, mangling the other leg as well.

I was mummified in plaster from the waist down, and for the rest of the school year I remained at home, itching and sweltering in my stinking cast.

My little brother was four or five years old then, and I used to badger my parents when they didn't know where he was. What was he doing outside? Didn't they know that there were cars out there, roaring up and down the street?

The logic of catastrophe became total. When the improbable happens its probability becomes a hundred percent, and you find you can't force it back into the normal distribution. Who cares about the normal distribution anyway, when the worst has already happened?

The cast was removed in May, and for three weeks my soft, scarred legs were strapped into braces. But even after these too had been

1

removed, and I no longer needed my crutches to get around, I was terrified of venturing out of the house. So I holed up in my room, watching the cars cruise the street below like sharks.

I may have found safety at home, but not much peace. My father, Richard Osborne, was a refugee from upper-class Boston who had set out at an early age to fail the family's expectations.

Those expectations had thwarted a lot of Osborne men before him. Grandpa Osborne's passion at Harvard had been anthropology, but at the turn of the century the Osbornes equated professors with bootblacks and snake-oil salesmen, and so academia was out of the question. Grandpa spent his life unhappily as a banker and eventually tried to run his two sons through the same gauntlet: Exeter, Harvard, and a place in the firm.

My father got as far as Harvard, veered off to Pomona, and then returned East to open a bookstore in the suburbs of Philadelphia. He had real contempt for Boston, and all his life he stayed angry at it. He was worshipping James Dean when I was nine, and I couldn't understand it. I used to wonder, *Why are we going to see* Rebel Without a Cause *for the fifth time, and why is my father crying?*

My mother had graduated cum laude in physics on a Radcliffe scholarship, and when she quit her first job to follow my father South she'd been earning the unheard-of wartime salary of $30,000. Her sacrifices and his profligacy were the interlocking themes in the pathology of their marriage, and many nights my brother and sister and I would fall asleep to the cacophony of my parents' exchanges.

As a boy I could never understand what it was that so enraged my father. Sometimes it seemed to be Grandma Osborne, though Dad had always been the old lady's favorite. Sometimes it seemed to be my mother, though she had given up everything to keep his business going during his breakdowns and binges. And sometimes we children would wonder if it was us, until my father would pause from his furies and speak to us so tenderly that for a time he seemed capable of infusing good feeling into the entire universe.

My father was the source of the chaos and pain in my family, but he was also capable of great warmth, and like so many Osborne men he had a strong maternal instinct. My cousin Tod is about the only other father I know besides myself who wishes he could lactate. In this day and age it seems to be all right to have those feelings, but for the preceding generations they were shameful. My grandfather and my father and his brother, Uncle Henry, didn't know what to do with them, and you never knew as you came into their presence whether to expect tenderness and ebullience or depression and rage.

In late June of 1956, my parents shipped me off to Alden, Massachusetts, to spend the summer with Uncle Henry, my father's older brother, in the family summer compound on the shore.

Known in the family as the "Peaceable Kingdom," the compound consisted of fifty acres of woods, fields and wetlands set on a point Grandpa Osborne had purchased for a song at a municipal auction in the 1940s. Uncle Henry had inherited the family home, an 1835 farmhouse that had been attached to various converted outbuildings by means of enclosed porches and walkways. The living room occupied half of the downstairs and was filled with mementoes from the family's maritime days: scrimshaw, harpoons, sailing prints, Chinese chests, and vases.

It has always seemed to me that for charter members of America we Osbornes don't have a hell of a lot to show. Our branch of the Osbornes had come over on the Mayflower and had had three hundred years to buy land, amass fortunes, exploit workers, acquire power and generally make a splash, and yet what power and fortune we could still claim had been mostly acquired by marriage.

In the early 1800s a seafaring Osborne named Isaiah married the daughter of a wealthy whaler who set him up in business providing capital and canvas to China traders. Isaiah made a success of it eventually, acquiring several clipper ships of his own along the way. On his death in 1861 Isaiah's business fell to his son James, a Utopian who tried to organize the firm around worker housing, worker welfare and profit-sharing, as an enlightened response to the incipient labor movement of the time. By all accounts James Osborne's workers loved him, and he loved his workers, and by 1879 he'd just about bankrupted Osborne Sheets and Canvas.

That would have been the end of the family fortune if it hadn't been for his widow, Clara, whose wealthy bachelor brother left her his fortune on his death in 1883. By the 1930s the family portfolio, consisting primarily of bonds and real estate, was still substantial, and on the death of Grandpa Osborne in 1952 the patriarchy fell to my Uncle Henry.

Uncle Henry Osborne was the supreme protector of our diffident clan, and in its cause he was a dragon. Large, rumpled and dyspeptic, he seemed always to be on the verge of exploding. He had lived on his wits in the board rooms of Boston, and when his wits failed him he resorted to intimidation, shaking his jowls and pounding his great pink fists and shouting, "In a pig's ass," his favorite expression. Like my father, he was capable of real tenderness, but it was random; niceness would strike with the reliability of lightning.

Thanksgivings and Christmases at Uncle Henry's house were patriarchal rituals, as ceremonial and obeisant as the wedding in *The Godfather*. He intoned the grace and dissected the turkey and enforced his expectations from the oaken baronial throne he used to occupy at the head of the dining table. Everyone from his children to his in-laws was in awe of him, and whether they wanted to buy a house or get married or send their children to prep school he would lead them into his sepulchral library and listen as they made their case, stirring his martini and puffing on a Churchillian cigar.

You would tell him what you wanted to do and wait as he worked a bit of tobacco off his tongue or plucked the cocktail onion from his toothpick, and a part of you would wait him out, and pray he would okay it, and another part of you would be thinking, *Well, what if he doesn't okay it? Who gives a damn?*

But no one refused to perform these rituals because Uncle Henry did his duty, which was to do battle with the forces of darkness for the rest of us Osbornes and protect posterity from the ruin to which we seemed so naturally inclined. After all, he was the sole Osborne in anything that could pass for business; none of the rest of us even knew exactly what it was he did. In fact, a cultivated ignorance of the Osborne estate seemed to be as much a part of our bargain with Uncle Henry as the rituals and obeisances.

I'd been raised to believe that misfortune was ennobling, but by the time I arrived in Alden my convalescence had turned me into an overbearing little brat. Everyone had been so happy that I'd survived, and I had been so immobilized by my cast, that I'd grown accustomed to the universe hopping to it at the snap of my fingers.

Like a good little ambassador I contrived to represent my family's pathology when I arrived in the Peaceable Kingdom, and as I hobbled around the compound I affected my father's contempt for everything Bostonian. I was disdainful of my cousins and used to sit apart, reading Melville on the lawn that sloped down to the shore. But the family wasn't in the least impressed; they'd seen it all before.

My cousins began to dub me "Aunt Tom" for my inertia, but Uncle Henry, for all his bluster, abided by his nephew. He had no sons at the time, so I became his little boy, and he was like a father to me.

The Osborne men weren't very gifted at having fun until they had families of their own. Children became the agencies of their recreation, so it was always more a matter of the men pulling the children along than vice versa. Fortified with Bloody Marys, Uncle Henry would charge out into the compound each morning like a liberated bull and drag me away from my books and send me shinnying up the mast on my aching legs to rig his sailboat, a thirty-foot sloop he'd dubbed the *Clara*, after my great grandmother, the family benefactress. Then off we would sail together, waving to the women on the shore as we tacked into Vineyard Sound.

Some evenings we would fish in vain for blues in the tide off the point, with Uncle Henry puffing on his cigars and cursing his unaccommodating prey as he cast far out into the gloom. And one day he took me in to Boston to the Osborne box at Fenway, where he cursed himself hoarse at the feckless Red Sox, crushing his hotdog in his fist as yet another Yankee rounded the bases. And every night he would appear in my room and settle into the creaking wicker chair by the window and read to me from Twain and Dickens and Kipling, his voice rising and falling and rising again with the fortunes of Huck and Oliver and Kim.

So under Uncle Henry's firm hand I staggered back out into the world that summer, and by September I'd lost my invalid flab racing full tilt around the Peaceable Kingdom.

———————

I attended public school through the fourth grade, but from the fifth grade on my mother sent me to private school. My father refused to consider sending me to boarding school, however, and so I attended Whitney Country Day, a local academy that fed its boys to Princeton and Penn State.

Up to the time of the accident I'd been unhappy at Whitney Country Day. It was an extremely cliquish school, and I got sorted very quickly into the meatball category, maybe because I was always reading and talking about books. One way or another people sensed that I was different somehow. Being a meatball meant that it was always open season for abuse from top and middle management. It meant that you were always a fullback on the soccer team, and basically stood around with the other meatball fullbacks, doing nothing.

During my invalidism I had convinced myself that the accident would permanently fix me in the meatball category, and as if to bear me out, I was immediately accosted after the first soccer practice in September by the Waverly twins, a pair of tow-headed rich boys who were pretty high up in the pecking order.

With the same kind of confidence with which some cracker might tell a black that he couldn't move into the neighborhood, the Waverly boys blithely informed me that they hated me and that generally speaking my existence lowered the quality of their lives.

So before I knew it I had jumped both of them at once, and we had one of those fights kids have: rolling around and banging each other with our arms and so on. It was all pretty ineffectual, but it did good things for me; I wasn't so much of a meatball after that. In fact, I became something of a romantic figure at Whitney Country Day, and by senior year my schoolmates had elected me president of the class.

Academically I was less triumphant. I had always been a bad student, but I don't think that the markings of a true academic failure began to emerge until the sixth grade.

I was facile in English and history and social studies because for me they required no study. If I heard it or read it I knew it. I had no problem as long as the material could be turned into a story because stories were intrinsically interesting to me. As a consequence I don't think I figured out what the process of learning was until I was in my thirties. I thought all I had to do was sit down and read about the Peloponnesian War and then tell somebody about it: no sweat. I didn't understand why the same thing didn't happen when I read algebra; I just figured there was something wrong with me. I didn't realize that what was wrong with me was that I wasn't working.

The guidance counselor advised me to apply to Denison, Wake Forest, and Marietta, but instead I applied to Harvard, Princeton, Yale, and (on the advice of my English teacher) Oberlin, figuring that if I applied only to the best schools one of them would have to take me.

People thought I was crazy because my grade record was so bad. I never passed a math course after the sixth grade and had to get special permission to graduate.

The admissions officer at Harvard said, "What are you doing here? Are you completely out to lunch?" His counterpart at Princeton was a friend of one of my teachers, but he couldn't swing it either, and I completely bombed at Yale.

But the man I talked to at Oberlin was head of admissions, and we had a long chat about the books that I'd read and about Melville and Conrad and world peace and all that.

He admitted me on the spot, purely on the basis of my being a good talker. Of course it was a big mistake on his part because the scores were right. I would have done better at some little half-assed school where they might have given me the support I needed. The real problem with me was that I was too pissed off to go to school, too angry to sit in one place and think about anything besides myself.

When I left for Oberlin in 1963 my father finally chucked his bookstore completely and moved my mother and my kid brother and sister to a ramshackle house on Siesta Key, Florida, where he died a few months later.

The store hadn't been doing well. Toward the end my mother had basically kept it going. My father had made a mess of everything. But no matter how much he'd let his customers down, they were still devoted to him, and it has always amazed me how much people will put up with from somebody so long as they know he cares about them. But it was the same way with us. He had let me down, too, and he'd made a mess of my mother's life, and he outraged the family up in Boston. But we had loved him because we knew he was in such pain.

I suppose it would not startle a psychiatrist to learn that I spent a lot of my youth fixing on older men, looking for someone to admire and believe in. There had been Uncle Henry himself, first and foremost, whose influence, whether direct or oblique, continued to be potent. Then at Whitney Academy it had been my English teacher, an acerbic iconoclast named Chamberlain who'd steered me from Melville to Conrad.

At Oberlin I was taken under the wing of an emeritus historian named Miller who'd admired an essay of mine on my Utopian Uncle James and steered me through and around calculus and poet's physics and focused my attention on his specialty, the abolitionists. It was a turbulent time for the college, but out of either an historian's detachment or a preppie's diffidence, I kept my distance from a lot of the demonstrations that gathered on Tappan Square.

I never looked for big trouble in school. I was angry, but that didn't mean I wanted anger heaved back on me, so if I was antiauthoritarian it was as a kind of guerrilla. And in fact I still don't like being in trouble; it undermines my self-confidence. To be in trouble makes me wonder whether maybe I *should* be in trouble, and that takes a lot out of me.

So I wasn't a revolutionary. I was mildly defiant toward some of my teachers, but it mainly got acted out as an identification with the beatniks of the 1950s. Beatniks didn't behave badly. They tended to be a little contemptuous and cerebral, but they didn't vandalize anything.

I lived off campus my junior and senior years, and spent my days in the library and the snack bar cultivating infatuations with a series of Oberlin belles. Whitney Country Day hadn't prepared me for female society. I always hankered after the most rebellious girls on campus, but I could never really meet their gaze. I thought what you were supposed to do was impress females by being totally autonomous—like Gary Cooper, perhaps. I never understood that if you acted as if you were totally autonomous you were really telling them, "Who needs *you*?" So I never got anywhere.

After I graduated from Oberlin in 1967 I followed some friends into the VISTA volunteer program. I'm not sure why. My friends had joined primarily to avoid the draft, but I'd gotten a deferment on account of my legs, which still looked fragile in X-rays. Perhaps I saw VISTA as a way of getting out into the world.

I was assigned to teach history in a black neighborhood in Providence, Rhode Island, but due to staff cutbacks I found myself teaching mathematics instead. Fortunately I was assigned to the slowest kids in the school, so I could keep them down at my level almost perpetually. But it didn't take long for the principal to realize that I wasn't cut out to be a teacher.

The principal was a maverick named Herman Stack who'd been assigned to the school as punishment for his opposition to the Commissioner of Education's consolidation scheme. Stack recognized a fellow misfit when he saw one and recruited me to help him develop an alternative plan.

It was going to be great. We were going to claim one of the abandoned mills around college hill and rework it into an experimental school with lots of emphasis on open classrooms and individualized instruction and day care and all the rest of it: very progressive, very community-based. The designs were terrific, and I got all whipped up about them. We got some architecture students from the Rhode Island School of Design to work on them with us, and when it came time for the hearing we marched in with all these plans and drawings.

Of course we were nuts to begin with because we'd never really trotted this out for the neighborhood and the commissioner had salted the crowd with parents who didn't want their kids going to school in some broken-down mill. So we were laughed right out of the hearing, and Stack resigned to become an educational consultant in Washington State.

I lived in a one-room apartment near the school. My neighbors had always been suspicious of me; they wouldn't have chosen to live in their neighborhood if they'd had a choice. But after the assassination of Martin Luther King they turned threatening. It got to the point where the black VISTA volunteer I'd been paired up with took me aside one day and told me to keep my distance so he wouldn't lose credibility with his students. I spent a couple of months more beating my head against the ghetto wall, but when Stack called with an offer to work with him out on the West Coast I was ready to go.

Washington State sounded exciting. I thought we'd be working in Seattle, or maybe at least Tacoma, but within a week or so I found myself moving in with Stack and his wife on a God-forsaken archipelago in Puget Sound called the Vaughn Islands.

The islands were a series of little rain forests, pristine and beautiful in their dank and somber fashion, but I didn't enjoy my time there at all. For one thing Stack caused a lot of tension because he wanted to fire all the old school marms and set up a new-fangled school. I became caught between the community and this educational madman. Stack was officially the administrator of a model-schools program that had been set up basically to burn up some federal money the state of Washington didn't know what to do with, and I was his assistant.

The islands were the last home of a little tribe of Indians called the Hanna, and they coexisted with a mix of Russians, Swedes and Irish, all leading rag-tag lives centered around the fisheries. I tried to see myself as a poverty worker, but it was hard to tell how poor people were because the culture itself was so downbeat.

A year after our arrival, Stack accepted a position in the nascent interactive-video industry and left me to fend for myself in the islands. At the age of twenty-four, I suddenly found myself head of a small and traumatized school system on the edge of nowhere.

A new governor came in around then whose campaign platform was aid to education. So I applied for a grant to develop the Vaughn Islands into a demonstration site for a new rural educational project. The grant came through, and our school became very lush, with lots of audiovisual equipment and performance space and all the rest of it because so much money had been thrown our way.

I ended up becoming something of a public figure, and I guess that's how I first came to the attention of the redoubtable Barbara Kaye.

2

BARBARA

It's strange, but even after everything we went through together—
the courtship, the marriage, the kids, the fights, the divorce, and
everything that followed—a lot of Barbara's life remains a mystery
to me.

I know that her father died when she was an infant. Her mother's
next husband had disliked children, and so all through Barbara's
childhood she'd been farmed out to relatives: aunts, uncles, grand-
parents, in a succession of houses stretching from Omaha to Albu-
querque. I know that after high school she followed an older man
named Stills to an oil field in Alaska, where she had a baby daughter
by him named Mag. And I know that Stills abandoned Barbara in
1971 and that she and Mag followed another man named Hampson
to the Vaughn Islands.

But that's about it. When I wonder why I know so little about my
first wife and the mother of my children, I have to remind myself
that for a long time I didn't say much about my life with Barbara to
Susan, my second wife. I always supposed that Susan didn't want to
know very much about Barbara, and for my part I wasn't exactly
bursting to tell Susan, either; Barbara was already a force in our life,
and I didn't want to give her any more power over us than she already
had. It would have been another intrusion on the life Susan and I
were trying to build together.

That's getting ahead of the story, I suppose, but what I suspect is
that Barbara didn't tell me much about her past because she was

afraid it might cost her our relationship. And for my part, I wasn't
in a retrospective frame of mind. My father had just died, and I
wanted to keep focused forward.

A friend of mine had us both over to dinner one evening. Barbara's
boyfriend Hampson came with her, but their relationship was obviously in a state of decline. He was the strong silent type, a depressed
ex-lumberman or something, and he seemed to recede as the night
went on. My friend, our host, was married, so naturally I assumed
that he'd invited Barbara and me in the hopes that we would hit
it off.

And we did. She took an interest in me, and I thought she was a
knockout. I couldn't take my eyes off her. She had a Gallic quality:
long black hair, a broad face with generous features, and a wonderful
smile. She had this way of looking at you full-face: very innocently,
the way a kid follows something, moving her whole head around,
not just her eyes. She seemed so unguarded and direct.

I kept trying to impress her all evening with how funny and smart
I was, playing off my friend. I was full of contempt for the bureau-
cracies I was dealing with and that seemed to strike a chord with
her. Every time I launched into another mordant anecdote I would
catch her staring at me with her eyes ashine.

Barbara was living on welfare and couldn't get a job without
finding day care for her daughter Mag, who was nearing her third
birthday. So she and a couple of other women were trying to set up
a day-care center. The trouble was that the families around the fishery
didn't like her plan. Mothers and grandmothers took care of the kids
if they got taken care of at all, and this day-care idea seemed to some
of them like an assault on their way of life.

Since I had developed some influence in the community she naturally approached me about it, and eventually her day-care project
became a reason for us to spend all day with each other, day after
day, and things moved along pretty rapidly. There wasn't any sense
in wasting time on the Vaughn Islands; if something was going to
happen you figured you might as well get started.

From the beginning our romance was stormy and painful. She liked
the anarchist she saw in me, the antiauthoritarian. She liked my anger,
I think. It wasn't that she wanted to see me miserable, and she

certainly didn't want my anger directed at her, but it reassured her when I was angry because she was angry about everything, and she wanted company. She liked to keep things mixed up, and I was always on my toes around her.

At that time in my life what I identified as love was an intense fear of loss. If I was scared to death, if I truly believed that I couldn't live without someone and was miserable with the anxiety of losing her, then that was true love for me; that meant I was really onto something good.

During our courtship, Barbara's daughter Mag and I sort of circled each other. It's important to understand that even though I'd backed into education I was not very good with children. My approach to them was abstract. I empathized a lot with them, and I had a bureaucratic sense of what they needed, but one-on-one I was uneasy with them.

I worked with Barbara on her day-care plan and helped her present it to the community at a meeting we'd set up together. It didn't go well. People were very hostile to the idea. Barbara didn't have her ducks in a row, and I didn't come to her rescue. Eventually she did get approval, but she was furious at me for leaving her to fend for herself in front of all those people, and I guess I figured she had a right to be. I felt ashamed of myself for retreating from trouble again. I could have done more to help her.

So we had a big fight, and soon afterward she came in and announced that if I didn't marry her she was going to leave the islands. That was always Barbara's way, dropping bombshells, declaring ultimatums. I don't remember if there had already been talk about marriage by that point, but I guess I was in pretty deep.

I wouldn't say I was adverse to the idea of marrying Barbara, but I was nervous. At that time I didn't know any happy marriages firsthand. I thought that the point of marriage was to lock yourself into a relationship that you didn't want to lose. I couldn't see anything positive about it in and of itself. So my reaction wasn't, *Great, we'll have a family*. Having a family wasn't part of my agenda; I don't think I even had an agenda.

I remember worrying that I wouldn't be a fit father for Mag. I didn't understand kids, and I didn't understand bonding. So we talked around this issue for a while, and then finally Barbara said, "Oh, well, we can always do something about Mag."

I said, "What do you mean, 'Do something'?"

And she said, "Well, we can always send her to my mother."

I said, "No, no. Never mind. We'll be fine." But I was astounded that she would do to Mag exactly what her own mother had done to her.

Then we went into this long negotiation that centered on the wedding date. I said we should wait a year; she said six months.

And all the time I was thinking, *Six months is plenty of time to deal with these things. Let's just get the noise down.*

That was my thinking all the way up to the wedding. I figured I had time to get out of it if I wanted to, but eventually I couldn't come up with a reason to get out of it. I couldn't honestly claim I had something better to do with my life.

In May I went East to pick up a wedding ring that my grandmother had left me. Uncle Henry was the keeper of the ring of course, so I went to his house in Boston. I don't think I wanted him to talk me out of marrying Barbara, but the whole courtship had occurred in such a vacuum that maybe I just wanted somebody at least to talk to me about it seriously.

But his reaction was, "Fine, great, wonderful." He'd never met Barbara of course, but he wanted me to have a family. He liked the idea on principle, and dashed up to the attic to fetch the ring. So I tied it to a string around my neck and flew back to the Vaughn Islands.

Barbara and I were married on June 18, 1974. In the Vaughn Islands a wedding is not merely a family event. The entire town turns out for it, with the crowd leaking through the fences toward the barbecue. None of the Osbornes attended, but Barbara's mother showed up with her most recent husband, an electrical-supply dealer named Stanley who had just retired to Colorado.

Barbara's mother had an eerily unscathed quality, like those mothers in the hand-cream commercials. At the wedding she outshone her daughter and swept through the gathering in an iridescent purple dress. There was never any question of my calling her "Mother" or "Mom"; everyone, even Barbara, called her Kitty.

I didn't like Kitty; she was picky and critical around Barbara. But I did like Stanley. He seemed to be genuinely concerned about Barbara and Mag, and took his paternal role seriously enough to take me aside before the wedding and grill me briefly about my prospects.

By then my prospects seemed dead-ended in the Vaughn Islands, and I had decided to resume my historical studies and enroll in a master's program at Harvard. My record at Oberlin had been as asymmetrical as my record at Whitney Country Day, and I'd been way over my head in the Vaughn Islands, but I looked like a fully integrated human being on my résumé, and I guess what they presumed to be my life experience put me over the top.

I don't know how serious I really was about history back then. I think what I was really doing was finding an excuse to go home. I was sick of the Vaughn Islands, and now I had this family to care for. I wanted a new beginning, but I also wanted to fold my new family into my old one. I wanted to impose some continuity on our lives.

On our way east I made a detour to Florida to introduce Barbara to my mother. At the time my mother was very unhappy. She hadn't forgiven my father for dying and leaving her down in Florida, so she was very cloying and clutching around her sons.

My mother hated Barbara from the start. I took everybody out to dinner, and she and Barbara had a debate about dieting or something, and at one point my mother took me aside and said, "I feel like throwing that woman down the stairs."

I was furious, and I told her so, but I tried to assume that my mother was merely jealous and didn't want to share her son with anybody. It wasn't until later that I found out that she believed that Barbara had married me for my money.

Uncle Henry offered us the run of a cottage in the Peaceable Kingdom, and my new family and I moved to Alden during the summer of 1975.

It was a little gray cottage with a lovely view of the bay, and at first Barbara was charmed by it. There were two bedrooms, a little kitchen, and a living room with a big stone hearth. The yard ran down to a hedge of beach plum, and then a little path took you down to the beach.

The family seemed to take to Barbara all right. She didn't instigate any major blowups those first years, and since the Osbornes never had any high expectations of getting along with one another, everybody thought she was fine.

I think Barbara respected Uncle Henry, and when we'd gather she would áct as his straight person, setting me up for the barbs he liked to toss my way out of his own peculiar brand of anguished affection. No matter how far along I got in life, Uncle Henry always had the effect of emulsifying me, and when we all gathered he liked to turn to Barbara and ask, "How do you put up with this character, kid? I mean, how do you ever wake him up in the morning and get him off to *work*?"

But Uncle Henry took stock of things pretty quickly and convinced me right away to adopt Mag legally. Since the family trust stayed in the family and never extended even to spouses, he was concerned that Mag wouldn't inherit anything if something were to happen to me. There was no question of notifying Stills, her natural father, because he'd completely disappeared from their lives. So I went to the Hammond County courthouse and made my paternity official.

I commuted to Harvard and my academic focus advanced chronologically—from the abolitionists to the Civil War to Reconstruction and finally to the mass immigrations of the late 1800s, where it remained. Up to that point in my life I liked to say about myself that I didn't suffer fools gladly, which really meant that I had no patience for anyone who didn't leap to conclusions as quickly as I did. Like my father, I'd always tended to believe that everyone else was put on this earth just to give me a hard time.

But the family steadied me, and I began to learn about studying. Immigration as a subject required that I learn statistics and demographics, and so I began to understand the difference between studying and reading, which was brand new for me, and strangely invigorating.

I'd never been so happy. I loved being married. Despite my doubts about fatherhood Mag did become a child of mine, and these feelings of being a family unit washed over me. Suddenly all those Osborne maternal instincts were unloosed.

Barbara must have been very confused, because she'd gotten married on one set of terms and then out of the blue came this whole other set of terms. She thought I was as much of a nomad as she was and now all of a sudden I started building a nest.

I'm sure she wouldn't have minded if I'd gone around feeling happy and fulfilled, as if I'd inherited a station in life. But what came with it was a set of expectations about how *she* should feel. These expectations had to do with our all working together to add to the cohesion and welfare of the family. It didn't matter to me what dimension that took. It didn't mean that she had to be a great cook or a perfect homemaker or any of that. It just meant that she had to contribute in spirit or labor with some kind of energy.

But Barbara simply didn't understand that. After what she'd gone through in her own childhood, that was all foreign to her. I was feeling like a family man, and I suppose she could have turned me in for false advertising, except that it was so inadvertent. I'd had no idea I had these feelings myself.

I loved being a father to Mag. She was five years old at the time and seemed to be flourishing in kindergarten. She developed a relationship with Aunt Jane, Uncle Henry's wife, and the Peaceable Kingdom seemed to acquire some meaning for her.

Things went so well with Mag and me that almost immediately I wanted more kids. I was discovering this capacity to care for children that I never knew I had, and it seemed to me all sweetness and light. More children would cement the bond between Barbara and me, and I wanted to populate the Peaceable Kingdom with children.

Barbara was against it at first. I don't know what her real reasons were, but the way she couched it at the time was that she wanted to take flying lessons.

I was buffaloed by this. It would have been all right if she'd said, "I want a career." But to begin with, what was she going to take flying lessons for? And why did having kids mean she couldn't take flying lessons? She already had Mag, and obviously she wasn't letting her stand in her way.

We had an awful fight, and at one point I blew up and ripped the towel rack off the bathroom wall. I never threatened her with it, but she got terrified and I too was scared by how angry I'd become. I became panicked; I didn't want to bully her, I didn't want to scare her away. So I realized the error of my ways and backed off, and she signed up for her goddamn flying lessons.

But then the fates must have intervened because a couple of weeks after that she announced she was pregnant. I guess the argument had scared some sense into both of us because we were good to each other for a long time after that. My relationship with Barbara during her pregnancy was great. For the first time we seemed to be immersed in the family together. The baby was due in early September, and Uncle Henry offered to invest $13,000 in an addition to the cottage. My cousin Tod, who had the next cottage over, helped me out, and we began work in the spring of 1976, building a nursery and an extra bathroom. It was great. I had this foolish pioneer feeling about the whole business, building a shelter before the winter came.

As it turned out we just made it. As I was nailing the last baseboard into place she began to have contractions, and I raced her off to the hospital in Hammond.

Barbara and I had attended Lamaze classes, but we were wrecks during her labor. The labor was long and hard and she got furious: screaming at me, at the doctor, at everyone who'd gotten her into this mess.

I was a lousy coach. I just wanted Barbara's pain to come to an end. I wanted somebody to do something. So they finally gave her Pitocin and she began having enormous contractions, and she kept screaming and cursing at me as they wheeled her off. I tried to follow after her, but the doctor on duty was an aging Italian who took a dim view of Lamaze and wouldn't let me in for the delivery. Barbara called my name and begged him to let me come with her, but I guess from his point of view I was worse than useless.

A nurse stayed with me in the hall, and once I'd calmed down a little she let me go to the door and look in the window. I got there just in time to see Sara emerge, smooth and calm and all business in the middle of this chaos.

My heart jumped at the sight of her. The doctor saw me and waved me in and suddenly everything was at peace. The doctor was smiling, and Barbara was smiling, and Sara seemed to be taking in the whole scene with pitying comprehension. I felt as if a fever had broken.

3

THE CONVERSION

That night I went all through the cottage, arranging things for Sara, setting up the little nursery I'd built so that there would be something to catch her eye everywhere she looked. I felt exalted, jubilant, and I could not sleep. Uncle Henry came by to keep me company, and as Mag slept with Aunt Jane up in the big house we got a little smashed together, killing a bottle of bad red wine and singing *Million-Dollar Baby* in two-part dissonance.

Mag was five going on six when Sara came along, and she seemed pleased to have a sister. I think that as far as she was concerned anything that kept her mother in one place for a little while was to be encouraged, but there was more than that to her affection for Sara. She cooed at her in the visitor's room at the hospital and marveled at Sara's tiny features: her minute fingernails, her dimpled chin, the faint haze of reddish hair on her soft, pale skull.

Barbara recovered quickly from the delivery, and within a couple of days she and Sara returned to the cottage. I had prepared the nest as best I could, but as soon as she got back Barbara decided that even with the addition I'd built, the cottage was too small for the three of us. Besides, I would have our only car at work, and she was concerned she would be too isolated out on the point. So she demanded that we rent another house closer to town.

Naturally this pissed off Uncle Henry. He'd spent $13,000 on the addition, and now Barbara was rejecting it. I felt lousy about it too, but to keep the peace I gave in, and Uncle Henry rented the cottage out to a Canadian named Bruce Smythe.

It seemed to Uncle Henry downright perverse of us not to live within the Osborne compound. And though we moved into a house closer to town, it turned out to be even lonelier than the cottage because by the end of September all of our neighbors had vacated for the winter. I remember we had an ice storm that February, and for several days the power was off, and we all had to huddle together next to the fireplace like something out of Laura Ingalls Wilder. Barbara absolutely refused help from Uncle Henry and even from Smythe, our successor in the cottage.

But despite our isolation the four of us were happy that first year. I used to lay Sara across my stomach when she had colic and put her to sleep singing "Jacob's Ladder."

My work went well. Barbara was spread thin, and I used to have to double up on the housework as soon as I got back from Cambridge, but I didn't waste my energy so much trying to figure out who was going to screw me over next.

As my paranoia receded a little, my work on immigration began to take hold. I found a community of Cape Verde Portuguese near Alden and centered my studies on them, spending my mornings out on the boats and docks, coaxing stories from fishermen as they mended their nets. I was the first in my class to finish my final paper, and in June of 1977 the family gathered to see me march up to receive my master's.

That September, precisely on Sara's birthday, Barbara gave birth to Benjamin Huntington Osborne, a keen, redheaded ringer for Great Uncle Henry. The delivery this time was easier, but Ben came forth howling: a small, livid fist of a baby whose first act in the outside world was to pee on his father.

As far as Barbara was concerned, this pregnancy had been as unintentional as the first, but there was no accounting for fecundity, and she was as pleased as I with our latest creation. Ben unfolded before us like the opening of a flower those first days, and for all his newborn bluster, by the end of the week he had cast off his great-uncle's mask for a compact version of his sister Sara's.

After I received my degree I'd begun looking for a job, but the household wasn't flourishing. Barbara had a hard time getting out of bed some mornings, and a lot of domestic business was going begging. One evening I was sitting out with Uncle Henry on the lawn, and he told me that if he were in my place he would stay home a while and help Barbara with the kids. I didn't like the idea of interrupting my work now that I felt I had some momentum built up behind me, but it seemed the right thing to do, so for about six months I stayed home and helped out.

Marriage may have changed my relationship with Barbara, but being a father changed me completely. It gave me a real sense of having a piece of the rock. I wasn't just stewing in my own juices anymore. Suddenly I was attentive, my antennae were out. I was involved in something beyond myself that was nonetheless an extension of myself, and I just reveled in those babies: up to my neck in diapers and feedings and all the rest of it.

I wanted to steep them in Alden, and I used to go marching around the Peaceable Kingdom with Mag at my side and Sara on my hip and Ben joggling along on my back, showing them all the sweet, beautiful things life had in store for us.

In early 1978 I was offered a position with a consulting firm in Vermont that was devising oral history programs for public schools. It seemed an interesting project, and the position was a nice blend of my experience in the Vaughn Islands and my study of the Cape Verde fishermen.

I'd had an interesting pair of years at Harvard, but I'd felt cut off from the world, and this seemed to me a nice way of working my way back into it. Barbara was for it, because the job was at Bourne College in Vermont. She felt isolated in Alden, where the winter population was reduced to a few fishermen and retirees. She wanted to get away from the Osborne clan and live in a college town, and I guess that for all my attachment to the Peaceable Kingdom, I was ready for a move as well.

When the Bourne firm sent me a contract I showed it to Uncle Henry and he was very downbeat about it. He pronounced it a rinky-dink job for someone with a Harvard degree, and from his reading of the fine print it looked to him as though the whole job could disappear in six months when the funding ran out. I got pissed off, figuring he just didn't want me to take the kids away. I told myself it was about time I stood up to the old man and made my own way.

So I signed the contract, and we moved to Bourne. We found a nice house a couple of miles out of town and a good school for Mag. I liked my job. It involved trying out our program on some local high-school kids and guiding them around homes for the elderly, where they interviewed people about their childhoods. One time we found a man who claimed to have crossed the country in a covered wagon as a child, been wounded in a gunfight in Laramie, Wyoming, and come back to New England to help out his family during a mill strike in the Twenties. He was one of the most gifted liars I ever heard, nevertheless I could see those kids' brains lighting up as he told his stories.

But Uncle Henry had been right; after six months the funding did dry up, and I was out of a job. So I wound up taking an even lower-grade position conducting research at Bourne for a history professor: a knee-jerk revisionist named Borden who was very big on medical explanations for everything: Lincoln had Marfan's syndrome, bread mold accounted for the Salem witch trials—that sort of thing.

I didn't like Borden, and I didn't like what he did with my research. But I was learning a lot. I'd been a very late developer and had to learn some very basic stuff. After I'd learned about bonding and nesting and human feelings, I had to learn about work.

So I sank my teeth into the job, and after a few months as a researcher I was offered a position as an instructor at Bourne, and I was initiated into the academic life. I found that I enjoyed teaching college students. This need I'd always had to turn everything into a story worked well in the classroom, and I began to find a place for myself in the department as a sort of counterpoint to revisionists like Borden.

I was getting better and moving along. When something didn't go my way I didn't tip over or fall apart; I had the ballast of my family. It gave me stability and with that came a kind of serenity, or at least composure, and I stopped antagonizing people so much. I made friends, alliances, progress.

———

I thought I was changing for the better, so it was frustrating when Barbara didn't seem to move with me. Barbara had shared my problems with authority; they had been a bond between us. And now she was rankled that I was beginning to make a little peace with it. She still wanted me to be alienated and nomadic. She still wanted everything fluid, the way things were when we first got together.

After I got the instructorship she started to revert to her flying-lessons mode again. She kept declaring all these ambitions, and the thread that ran through all of them was being famous and fearless and adventuresome. A lot of these ambitions were in the arts. She was going to be a ballet dancer. She was going to be a painter. She was going to be a poet. She was going to be a poet *and* a painter *and* a ballet dancer.

It seemed to me that these were perfectly normal fantasies for a teenager, but at some point you give them up. You fill yourself with the importance of your work or your family, and the need for fantasy fades away.

What frustrated me was that she would announce all these ambitions, and then she would just sit there and not do anything about them. The sticking point for me was that as far as I was concerned she couldn't say she was doing something when she wasn't, and after a while I became a real taskmaster in that sense. "What are you going to *do*, Barbara?" I used to ask her as she hung around the house. "You can't just sit here all the time."

She felt that I was putting her down, that I was attacking her character. I didn't think I was. I thought maybe I was being a disciplinarian sometimes, talking to her like she was a kid: "Now Barbara, you can't just fantasize."

But I didn't mean to imply that she couldn't do anything. I just meant to remind her that if she was going to use up family resources, there had to be a product. You couldn't just call yourself a poet and never write any poems.

Lurking under all this, of course, was a specter from my boyhood. My mother had been extraordinarily accomplished when she'd met my father, and my father had taken it all away. I was determined that I wasn't going to do that to Barbara. Whatever it was she said she was going to do, I was going to insist that she really do it, that she actually accomplish something. I couldn't let her disappear into a dream world.

This conflict developed gradually. At first when we moved to Bourne I thought we were really in business. Ben and Sara and Mag seemed to go from strength to strength, and Barbara was excited by the college. She signed up for a writers' group and produced some poems that I thought were great.

But I kept waiting for the family to come to represent to her what it meant to me, and it just never seemed to. She wasn't deriving anything from it. It seemed like an obstruction to this romantic vision she had of herself.

After she wrote those poems I offered to convert a room in the house into a studio for her. It involved ripping out some old plaster and applying a four-by-eight piece of sheetrock to the ceiling. By the time I'd carted the plaster away the house was full of dust. When I asked Barbara to help me hoist the sheetrock up so I could nail it into place she refused and stood by as I fashioned a brace out of a two-by-four to hold up her end. And as I wrestled the sheetrock upward I remember thinking, *Osborne, you're in this all alone.*

Once the room was finished it did seem to help Barbara's output a little. She would alight there occasionally and try to do some work. She even got started on a novel, but she tore up everything she started, and after a couple of weeks she dried up.

Finally, one day she told me that what she really needed was a room of her own. I asked her what was wrong with the room she already had, but she said she'd been reading Virginia Woolf, and she realized she couldn't work at home any more because she was distracted by a dirty house and dirty laundry.

I didn't understand. Virginia Woolf wanted her to have a room of her own, so she moved her literary gear out of the house and rented a room in town.

In what I presumed to be her splendid isolation she developed a fascination with the Holocaust, and by the fall of 1978 I was coming upon books on Auschwitz and Babi Yar scattered around the house among the rattles and sponge blocks.

At dinner parties and family gatherings Barbara's conversation grew more and more apocalyptic. She took to bringing every subject to its most grotesque extension: one minute you thought you were talking with her about chicken salad, and all of a sudden you were on hormone-ridden feed grains, famine, and vivisection.

I regarded the Holocaust as the central horror of modern history: the grotesque macrocosm of the worst that people can do. The professor in me couldn't do much of anything about what amounted to her intellectual terrorism. The sheer dimension of the Holocaust trivialized everything that was happening in our own lives: especially its sweet and modest satisfactions. But it seemed to click with Barbara's apocalyptic take on the universe, and one day she came to me and announced that she was going to convert to Judaism.

She never really explained why. I assumed she just felt like it. She hadn't shown the slightest interest in religion before that, and in retrospect I think that what she really had in mind was somehow becoming a Holocaust victim to validate her innate sense of righteous indignation.

When she announced this to me I said, "Just do me a favor, Barbara. Don't make me into a Nazi."

I remember thinking, *Well, this will just about finish off Uncle Henry.* But her conversion was all right by me. To my own way of thinking the infinite didn't seem to matter very much, but my attitude was that anyone in her middle thirties was free to decide on a religion.

We all took part in the conversion one way or another. I would help her with her memorizations, and there would be ceremonies at dinner: the lighting of candles and so on. The kids enjoyed a lot of it. I didn't take on patriarchal functions, but I rolled with the punches and stood up for her when my Jewish friends in the college began to imply that my wife was *meshugah.* To them being Jewish wasn't anything you could convert to, any more than you could convert to being Chinese.

Rabbi Shapiro from the college took an interest too. At first he was reluctant and bewildered, but eventually he was convinced by her seriousness and devotion, and in the end he went out on a limb for her.

But when Barbara started becoming Jewish she also found this itinerant Israeli in Mount Adams to teach her Hebrew. He was a great big handsome fellow named Elon, and she was always driving over to Mount Adams to have her sessions.

This was beginning to make me very insecure because I remember feeling as though she was going to leave us, as though there were nothing at home that she wanted. I guess part of my anger about her room of her own was that I saw it as a trysting place.

I don't really know what her relationship was with Elon, but it made me very nervous. It made me feel probably the same way my job at Bourne made her feel: excluded, alienated, as if all the nourishment were coming from somewhere else. What was good in my life was my work and my children, and what was good and exciting in her life was becoming Jewish and learning Hebrew, and we didn't share any of it at all.

Her conversion was at a temple in Brookline. The rabbis who presided were not old men with black hats and beards, but they were pretty conservative. Rabbi Shapiro accompanied us and presented Barbara's case. They listened very politely at first, but as soon as they realized that I wasn't a Jew and that Barbara was doing this on her own, they became agitated.

"What are you doing to us, Morris?" they asked poor Rabbi Shapiro. "We can't turn this lady into a Jew."

The oldest of them told Barbara that he could understand her attraction to Jewish culture, but why couldn't she just enjoy that? Why did she have to get involved in the actual religion?

His argument was that if they wouldn't marry their best friend's child out of the religion, how could she ask them to *create* a mixed marriage? The highest duty of Jewish women was to maintain the religion—how was Barbara supposed to do that when the rest of the family wasn't Jewish?

Shapiro and Barbara were so crushed they were speechless, and I could see the color rising in Barbara's cheeks. She'd worked so hard at this, come so close to finally transforming one of her fantasies into reality, that I was afraid of what she might do if they turned her down.

Suddenly I found myself raising my hand and asking if they would hear me out. They all nodded at me, as though it were a relief to have somebody say something, and I stood up and engaged them in a little debate.

My argument was that their obligation not to dilute the tribe only held when they were marrying someone who was Jewish to someone who was not. But in this case it was a matter of letting somebody who was not Jewish *into* the tribe. I figured that the rabbis were only constrained once Barbara was Jewish, so at this point why weren't they free to decide however they wanted?

They thought this was a very Talmudic argument, and there was a lot of shrugging and muttering among them. Finally they all looked at each other, and the eldest said, "All right, let's admit her." And that was that.

Barbara nearly fainted with relief, and I remember Shapiro turning to her on the way to the rites and saying, "Your husband must love you a lot."

And I did love her a lot, but we just kept pulling apart. Barbara was given the ritual bath, and we had a celebration back home, but we were still moving in different directions.

I entered a depressed period during which I would get up and go to work, come home to a spare and grudging supper, and after doing the dishes and tucking the kids into bed I would retire to my study and lose myself in my work. Then, around eleven o'clock, after Barbara had gone to bed, I would sit myself down in front of the television and drink beer, dozing off like a couch potato to the murmur of Carson and Koppel and the late-night movies. I felt as though I were losing my grip on the family rock and there was nothing I could do about it.

I kept trying to lure Barbara back into the family, to see if I could capture her imagination again with the kids and me. But too often I'd get frustrated, and these seductions would break down into lectures and recriminations. Why was Mag late to school again? Where were the bills Barbara was supposed to pay? Why wasn't there any milk in the house?

As far as Barbara was concerned all this harping was like flies in summer. She told me I was driving her crazy, that I had no conception of the ordinary give and take between human beings.

Finally, in the middle of one of our arguments, she told me that if I didn't get some help she would divorce me. Another declaration,

another ultimatum. If *I* didn't get any help *she* would divorce *me*? I
didn't like the way that was framed. I wasn't going to climb up on
a couch with a gun to my head.

But then later I felt more and more compelled to have a witness.
When I talked to Barbara and told her how I felt about the family
and the children and work, she didn't understand what I was talking
about. Nothing I said had any validity for her, and we invariably
ended up fighting. So I guess I began to see therapy as a chance to
take my case before a third party and have somebody in authority
say, "Barbara, listen to this guy. He's right."

We found a counselor named Irene Stone. She was a woman, she
was Jewish, and she seemed like a great idea to both of us. I figured
Barbara would find her sympathetic, and I might get my case heard.
But by then we were already pretty far gone as a couple.

We took turns telling our sides of the story to Irene. Barbara told
her I was emotionally crippled. In the eight years of our marriage
she'd never heard me laugh, she said, and she had seen me cry only
once, at a showing of *The Pawnbroker*. I was controlling and paternalistic, with the narrowest possible view of family life, and now,
to cap it all off, I was drinking beer into the late-night hours. Irene
listened to all this and asked if I thought that perhaps I was too rigid.
So then I launched into my side of the story and halfway through
my soliloquy Barbara jumped up and accused Irene of siding
with me.

By the spring of 1980 we were a shambles and a botch. After the
second visit to Irene, Barbara refused to return, and I started going
alone, just to hold myself together. When the time came for our
annual trip to Alden, Barbara announced that she wasn't coming
with us, and for two weeks I made excuses for her, for myself, for
the whole sorry mess we were making of our life together.

She did come down eventually, but one morning when we were
in bed together she said, "You know, my lawyer says that if we get
divorced I can get half of the land over here and half of the trust."

I didn't even know that she had a lawyer, but evidently she'd found
this woman they called the Muleskinner because she stripped hus-
bands of everything they were worth, and Barbara had shown her
all my documents.

"Are you kidding, Barbara?" I said to her. "You can't have any of that. It's not mine. It belongs to the trust."

That obviously threw her, but I didn't press the advantage. I was trying to handle the subject of divorce as lightly as possible, hoping it would disappear.

So I took her out to dinner that evening, and I guess in a way I belittled the divorce by trying to be calm and glib about it. But I just didn't believe it myself. I figured it was just another of Barbara's notions and that if I didn't fight back it might go away.

4

THE CHICKEN HOUSE

I was desolate, but I tried to figure that divorce was just something new Barbara had plucked out of the air. Everybody was getting divorced; it was part of the culture. People with weak egos become possessed by whatever's at hand—something on television or the last book they've read. So maybe these were just vibrations that she was responding to. She hadn't followed through on anything else, perhaps she wouldn't follow through on this.

Nevertheless, she'd set the ball in motion.

After we got back home to Bourne she said, "You have to leave."

Now, I thought the law had to be on my side. Surely the people who started divorce proceedings got the worst of it. No judge was going to throw me out of my own house.

"*I* don't have to leave," I said. "*You're* the one who wants a divorce. *You* have to leave."

But Barbara kept insisting, so I called this lawyer friend of mine, and I said, "Barbara's telling me that I've got to get out or she's going to have the marshal throw me out of my own house."

"I'm afraid she's right," he said. "It was a shock when it happened to me too. And I'm supposed to know about these things."

He told me that there was a no-fault system in Vermont. Divorcing couples didn't have to prove abuse or infidelity or drug addiction; all that was required was a separation. In order to guarantee Barbara's inalienable right to divorce me, the court was prepared to enforce a separation, and since mothers were almost always given custody of the children, and therefore the run of the house, it was up to me to clear out. It was a bind straight out of *Catch-22*, because if I didn't clear out I would be queering my case with the court with my intransigence, and if I did clear out I would be abandoning my children.

Finally the grimness of this thing started to sink in. I thought I'd been letting Barbara run, like a fish on a line, but it turned out it was the other way around. I couldn't believe it. All of a sudden she seemed to have the entire civil system at her disposal, and she was aiming it at me.

In less than two weeks I'd cleared out and moved to a little converted chicken house in Bourne. It was one of those sway-backed outbuildings done over in wallboard, with everything crammed under the eaves so you could only stand up straight in the middle.

The kids didn't take my departure too well. I picked them up every weekend, and they would come spend a day or two with me, but Ben was especially upset and clung to me when I dropped him off. Barbara waxed and waned at first, and after a month or so she began to couch our arrangement in terms of a trial separation, and we saw Irene Stone together again.

But it was the same thing all over again. Before long Barbara had decided that Irene and I were ganging up on her because, I suppose, Irene had had the audacity to tell her that I wasn't nuts. Barbara refused to continue seeing Irene, and in August of 1981 she announced that she was going through with the divorce.

Back before we were married I hadn't understood anything about family bonds. The idea that all of a sudden my life was going to be constrained by something the size of a loaf of bread was absurd to me, and I used to wonder, *What if it didn't love me? What if I didn't love it? What if for twenty-three years I had to feed, clothe, house and send to graduate school someone I didn't even like?*

But you entertain those fears when you're young, and then your children are born, and the world suddenly stops shifting underfoot. It's not enough to say that they're extensions of yourself, because in another way you become an extension of them as well. There's no use trying to explain the mysterious process of bonding, but the sense of original sin I'd carried around hangdog through my adolescence had given way to a sense of promise and redemption.

I'd always regarded my paternity as inviolable, but now someone who *wanted* the ground to keep shifting underfoot was going to take away my children. It had never occurred to me that anyone could do that. But it seemed as though this strange woman, who had only grown stranger to me the longer I'd been married to her, was going to take our children off with her into the vale of tears into which she was so determined to descend.

I found myself a lawyer, a phlegmatic young man named Bowles who had an office a block from my apartment. He told me that I couldn't get custody. The money was negotiable, we could talk about the house—but Barbara was going to get the kids.

I'd go to friends' houses and cry into their casseroles about how I was going to lose my family, and there was nothing I could do. But they tried to convince me otherwise: that things were changing, even in Vermont. I went to see my friend Sam Whitman, who was our family doctor, and his wife told me to go for custody. She'd been in the writers' group with Barbara, and they'd been friends until Barbara turned on her at one session, and now they couldn't stand each other. She told me I could get custody if I fought for it, but I was too demoralized to listen.

During my chicken-house period I would come to the house to get the kids, and sometimes I would just come up and stay there a couple of nights, as if to say, "All right, what are you going to do about it?" If Barbara made a fuss I would leave, but I was having a hard time separating.

We kept in touch one way or another. She would come down, and we would have lunch at Jimmy's, this greasy spoon near my apartment. I would try to act pretty gay about the whole thing because I figured that if she thought that she wasn't maiming me with the divorce she might lose interest.

One day we were having lunch, and all in one breath she said that she thought that I'd improved under Irene's care and that the kids thought I was better, too, so now she was going to move out of the house in town, and we were all going to move together into a brand new house in the country.

I was dumbfounded, jubilant. A reconciliation. Maybe we were going to survive after all. I moved some of my stuff back in and Barbara and I ran out and got a real estate agent. Within a week we'd bought this beautiful, restored brick farmhouse in Mount Adams. Barbara loved it and staked a claim to the attic study.

So all right, fine, things were going to be better. Everything was solvable. I would commute to work from Mount Adams, and everything was going to be great.

The house didn't have a washer and dryer, so after trying to figure out how to put together the finances and make the down payment and pay the month's rent on my chicken house and get a truck to move us, I said, "Let's put off the washer and dryer until my next paycheck. You can take the washing and drying to Bourne and put the stuff in and go to a bookstore or a restaurant and pick it up, and then we can get our own machines next month."

Well, she went batshit and demanded to know why everything had to come from her.

And I said, "What are you talking about, for Christ's sake? We're talking about three goddamn weeks."

So it was great: in two days we were supposed to move into the reconciliation house, and now we were arguing again, only this time I couldn't control myself, I couldn't pull any more punches. Why did everything have to come from *her*?

I told her that nothing had come from her since Ben was born. She didn't do anything. She didn't make any goddamn contribution. She lived in a dreamworld. She was deluded about who she was and what she was, and if we were going to have a reconciliation then things were going to have to be different.

She was very quiet after that, and the crisis seemed to pass. We proceeded with our plans for the reconciliation house, but on the very day we were to move she called me up and told me, "I'm not coming, Thomas." She was dropping my clothes off at Irene Stone's office, and the next person I would hear from was going to be her lawyer.

So that was that. The moving truck was idling in the driveway, packed with all our worldly goods, and the reconciliation, the marriage, was over.

That was so typical of Barbara. Somebody who has no sense of her innate power has to manipulate circumstances to punch people around. It's a kind of sleight of hand: mixing up people's lives to have an effect that you don't think you can have in and of yourself.

I moved into the house alone and began to fall apart at the seams. Ever since old lady Folkes ran me over I'd been afraid of the dark and afraid to be in a house alone, even in the daytime. I can't describe what it was like holed up in the reconciliation house. The dark just seemed to close in on me, and I'd run out of breath until I couldn't stand it any longer. One night I just ran out of the house and checked myself into a motel.

I was coming apart, and the craziness was bleeding all over the place. The kids were aware of all of it. Barbara and I worked out a kind of informal joint arrangement for Ben and Sara that lasted about three or four weeks. There were, in effect, two households, and the kids went back and forth, with rooms in both places. Sometimes there would be some late-evening decisions as to who wanted to go where, but generally Ben decided I needed him more than Barbara did, and so he stayed with me while Sara lived for the most part with Barbara and Mag.

Ben was depressed by everything, but Sara was funny; she dealt with life in a pretty straightforward fashion. She didn't get tackled by things. There was a lot of girl stuff, a lot of commiserating going on among Barbara, Mag, and Sara. They sort of hung together, and Ben wasn't taking part. He wasn't one of the gang.

Barbara finally decided that he should come live with me. I don't know if she decided that for her sake or his sake or mine. Maybe she did it because she thought I was going mad.

My craziness finally came to a head on their birthday. Ben was turning five and Sara was turning six, so Barbara arranged a party for them and sent me an invitation.

A couple of days before the party I'd had an indication that something was going screwy. I was trying to copy some things at the office, and when the Xerox machine wouldn't work I found myself wanting to tear it apart. I was just about to kick at the thing when I pulled myself back. *Slow down,* I told myself. *Take it easy. That's not like you.*

Then Mag came down to stay with me for the weekend. It had been a nice visit. Afterwards I was driving her back to Barbara's for Ben and Sara's party when I realized that for some time she'd been saying, "Dad? Dad?" and I hadn't been answering her.

"It's all right," I told her. "You can talk to me, Mag, but I just can't answer right now."

I began to lose my breath. I couldn't seem to muster enough energy to answer her. The steering wheel felt limp and useless, like a hoop of rope in my hands. I couldn't organize my thinking. I thought for sure I was finally going crazy. This was it. I'd lost everything else. Now my brain was gone.

We passed a hospital, and I had this tremendous sense of apprehension that something horrible was going to happen and I was going to be responsible. I was starting to black out, and I thought, *If I stop here on the highway I can run across the grass and get to the hospital and they can help me.* And then I thought, *But what if I don't make it?* And then I thought about the police. They could put me in a cell somewhere and call a doctor.

And all the while I'm saying to Mag, "Just keep talking, kid. But I can't answer you. I can't answer you."

It took all my concentration to keep driving, and I didn't think I was going to make it. In each town I kept telling myself to stop and get the police, find a hospital, call an ambulance. Something was about to pop.

Then suddenly we were at the house—I'd made it to the house. Mag got out, and I followed her a little way, but as soon as I heard the party through the door I knew I could never go in. Something critical was going on. A meltdown.

So I got back into the car and drove right to the hospital. I rushed into the emergency room, and I managed to tell the nurse that I needed help, that I needed a room. She read me right away and put me in this bright white room, and for the first time I felt safe. Whatever it was could come out now, and I would be safe.

The nurse sent for Sam Whitman, my doctor, and by the time he got there I was sobbing and keening and wailing. I must have gone on like that for an hour, two hours. I kept asking Sam if I was going to be all right, and he kept saying, "Yes, Tom. You're going to be all right. You're grieving. You're not depressed. Your ego's intact, your mind's intact." And after a while I believed him. I knew I was going to be all right.

After that I started to listen to my friends, and I decided to fight Barbara for the kids.

I began to see that there had always been something wall-eyed about her. In a way her problem was with depth perception, as though she herself were the only fully realized object she could perceive. It wasn't just that she regarded herself as the most important player in her life. As far as she was concerned, she was the only player on the whole stage. The rest of us were props. Over the course of her shuttled childhood she had somehow come to believe that she was infused with strange and wonderful powers—that she dazzled and haunted everyone who crossed her path. We had both mistaken my perplexity and my terror of losing our relationship for wonder and love.

Now that my bewilderment and fear had finally worn off, the first thing I did was sell the reconciliation house and move into an apartment in town.

Around this time Irene Stone told me about some Yale professors who'd written a book called *Beyond the Best Interests of the Child*. Their whole theme was that children should go to the nurturing parent in a custody dispute, whether that was the mother or the father. They were having a lot of influence with the courts and Irene encouraged me to hire these guys as consultants because she had concluded that I was the nurturing parent.

So I went back to Bowles, my lawyer, and he looked this stuff over and said, "Oh sure, we could probably get custody. She can't claim you're an unfit father now that she's handed Ben over to you for six months."

I felt like saying, "Look, asshole, why didn't you say so before?" But to him it was extraordinary that I wanted custody. It was as if he'd been saying, "What do you want the kids for? That's what's nice about divorce, isn't it? No kids." That seemed to be his attitude; maybe not personally, but as a professional, as an advocate.

In the meantime Barbara had fired the Muleskinner and hired a new lawyer: a man this time, named Fletcher. I don't know what went wrong with the Muleskinner, but Barbara always had a way of burning her bridges with anyone who found out too much about her. We had a session with Barbara and Fletcher, who blithely advised us in passing to read this new book he had found called *Beyond the Best Interests of the Child*.

Bowles and I looked at each other, and I said, "Read it? The authors are my legal consultants."

That had a real impact. Barbara's lawyer evidently told her later that the probability that she would win custody had shifted from 90 percent to 50 percent.

"We've got problems," he told her. "You've got a fight on your hands."

The business about the money she was after was getting tougher, too. Bowles and I were saying that we couldn't touch the trust, but in fact I suppose a judge could have said to me, "I don't care how you come up with the money, just come up with it." Nevertheless, we were crying poor.

So the whole business wasn't coming out as Barbara had hoped. I don't know what was going on in her mind during this period, but I think it had begun to occur to her that when it came to guaranteeing her survival maybe I was the only friend she had left.

Uncle Henry assured me that in the end I would get custody; that when it came to a choice between custody and money Barbara would go for the money, and then I would be rid of her for good. It was characteristic of Uncle Henry that because he wanted me to have the children he was utterly convinced that I would get them.

And in fact Barbara was running out of money. She had not tried in the meantime to get a job, and now her landlord was on her case. She was scared that she was going to lose everything on this gamble that she'd made.

When she asked about a settlement I would tell her, "Look, Barbara, of course you would get more money, and not only would you get more money, but the whole family would be grateful to you, and if you ever had money problems you could call Uncle Henry, and he would take care of you."

I meant it, too. I would go to bat for her. She was still the mother of my children, and I wasn't out to ruin her.

Barbara said it was logical for her to take Mag and for me to take Ben and Sara because she'd been out of the work force for ten years and couldn't support them all. But in retrospect I know that Barbara didn't cave in for the money. She settled for the same reason she'd pulled out of therapy—she didn't want to risk the exposure. The hearing alone would have been too terrifying for her. It would have played devastatingly on her adolescent fear that she wasn't really there. And she must have told herself that I wouldn't hold out long as a single father, that in the end I would come crawling back, begging her to take the children.

I considered fighting for custody of Mag, too. Her own father was completely out of the picture, and I worried about how all this was affecting her. But everybody told me that as merely an adoptive father I didn't stand a chance. Though Mag and I had been very close when she was younger, our relationship had been somewhat disturbed by Ben and Sara's arrival. As their natural father I had no doubt focused on them, probably to Mag's detriment. And then during the separation our relationship had not prospered. She sided with Barbara, and I was angry, and it was easy for me to lump Mag and Barbara together.

So on August 22, 1982, Barbara worked Grandma Osborne's wedding ring off her finger and handed it to me, and we signed the divorce agreement. I would pay Barbara $400 a month for Mag's child support until Mag reached her majority. If I lived more than a hundred miles from Barbara I would pay her up to $1200 a year in transportation costs. We would share school vacation time. I would pay $200 to Barbara for every month's time Barbara had visitation with the kids. I would pay $1,500 in charges she'd made on my American Express card. And I would pay Barbara three installments totaling $50,000.

In exchange for such considerations I became Ben and Sara's sole custodial parent.

5

THE LIFE RAFT

For all that, we continued to live as we had been living for the past year. My apartment was small and because of the settlement I couldn't afford anything larger for the time being. Ben came to stay with me, but Sara still shuttled to and fro between her brother and me at one end and her sister and mother at the other.

On a Monday in late September of 1982, a little more than a month after the ink had dried on our "Divorce Stipulation and Final Order," as it was elegantly titled, Barbara called to arrange to have lunch with me at Jimmy's, the little eatery that we had come to regard as neutral territory.

She had launched herself on a new diet involving a lot of roughage and now ordered a salad with no dressing. Her austerity somehow galled me, and I wound up ordering a double cheeseburger, a large order of fries, and a towering chocolate malted.

"Okay, Barbara," I said. "What's this all about?"

"Well," she said, "having lunch together doesn't have to be *about* anything, Thomas. But as a matter of fact—"

"Ah," I said.

"As a matter of fact, I do have some news."

"Okay," I said. "What kind of news?"

She got this wounded look. "Thomas, why do you have to be so hostile?" she wanted to know. "Can't we just talk?"

So I held my breath for a moment. "All right, Barbara," I told her. "I'm sorry. Tell me your news."

"Well," she said, straightening up and smiling. "Thomas, I'm going to Israel."

"Israel?" I said brightly. "Is that right? That's great, Barbara. How long are you going for?"

Barbara faltered a little then and narrowed her eyes. "You don't understand," she said. "I'm going to Israel to *live.*"

"To *live?*" I said. "What are you talking about?"

"Don't worry," she said quickly. "I'm not taking Ben and Sara."

"You're damn straight you're not taking Ben and Sara," I said. "But what are they going to do? How are they supposed to take this?"

She told me to get my voice down. "They can visit," she said. "And I'll visit them. I'm not abandoning my children."

"Then what do you call it, Barbara? How much farther away from them can you go?"

"I'm not abandoning my children!" she said, striking the table. "I have to do this. After all I've been through I need some time for me."

"For you, Barbara? You need some time for you?"

"And I have a friend over there. She's very ill. I have to be with her."

"Friend? What friend?"

"Listen, Thomas," she said. "Do you think this is easy for me? You're the one who demanded custody. Don't you *dare* suggest that I'm a bad mother."

I tried to catch my breath and glanced around the restaurant, meeting the gaze of several diners. "But what about Mag?" I asked Barbara. "What's going to happen to her?"

"She's coming with me," she said. "I'm going to enroll her in a boarding school in Israel. It'll be good for her. It'll be a wonderful learning experience."

Part of me wanted to say, "Jesus, Barbara, don't do this." But another part of me was already thinking, *Good-bye, Barbara. Maybe now Ben and Sara and I can get on with our lives.*

"All right, Barbara," I said. "All right. We'll make this work. We'll break it to the kids gradually. Work them toward it. I can take them on. I'll get a bigger apartment. All we'll need is time. When do you plan to go?"

"Sunday," said Barbara.

"Wait a minute," I said as she calmly forked her salad. "What do you mean, *Sunday? This* Sunday? Barbara, I'm *working*, for Christ's sake. How am I supposed to take them in by Sunday?"

"You know, Thomas," she said, "you can't expect everything to revolve around you. Things aren't always going to be as neat and tidy as you like them. A little more spontaneity could do us all a world of good."

I just gaped at her. "But you've given us only five days. How can we prepare Ben and Sara in five goddamn days?"

"I don't know what you mean exactly by 'prepare,' Thomas," she said. "I think you're underestimating our children. They're a lot stronger than you give them credit for."

End of conversation. I couldn't speak. I couldn't eat. I could only gaze in wonder at my former wife.

I wasn't around when Barbara broke her news to Ben and Sara, but it must have been as blithe and confounding a performance as she'd given at Jimmy's, because at first the kids took it lightly, as if mommies moved to Israel all the time. That was how Barbara always engineered things: dropping not just bombs but time bombs so she could be well clear by the time they exploded.

Ben was already pretty much settled into my apartment, so the main job was moving Sara's things from Barbara's house: clothes, toys, crayons, books, stuffed animals, all crammed into plastic garbage bags. By Wednesday Ben and Sara had laid claim to the bedroom and I had bought them a bunk bed and covered the walls with their drawings and maps and posters. Barbara's news had slowly sunk in by then, and Ben was growing grim and quiet, sitting at his desk and drawing tiny ships adrift on vast gray seas.

Sara, however, was clinging and manic, bubbling over about everything, as if it were all just terrific. I remember I handed her a new toothbrush for the move. She opened the box as if it were a Christmas present and gave me this shivering hug and told me that it was the bestest, most softest, and beautifulest toothbrush she'd ever gotten, and I was the bestest daddy in the whole wide world.

"Didn't I tell you?" said Barbara. "They're taking it wonderfully."

Barbara came by the apartment to say good-bye to the kids on Sunday evening. She took the children aside for their hugs and kisses and told them not to cry; she'd call and write and visit them and they would hardly know she was away.

Mag seemed to know better. It was she, not Ben or Sara, who broke down as the three of them embraced. I tried to say something positive to Mag as I embraced her; we were going to miss her, but she was so lucky to be going to Israel, it was a wonderful place, and she had to promise to write to us all about it. But she just stiffened in my arms and glared at me with those fierce, brimming eyes.

I tried to keep my distance when Barbara took her leave from Ben and Sara, and merely waved as she led Mag downstairs to the taxi. Sara and Ben went to the window and watched her drive off, and then they turned and looked at me, as if to ask me what was next.

I remember that I had decided ahead of time that the trick was going to be to keep everything as normal as possible for them, but somehow that first night I found myself buying them ice cream sundae suppers at the local gourmet creamery and taking them to a movie— something with Richard Pryor in it is all I remember, because I spent half of it in the men's room, cleaning up Sara, who had vomited her popcorn.

The next morning I tried to find my footing again. I got up around six, and by the time the kids woke up I had breakfast ready: one of those picture-book breakfasts you see on the back of cereal boxes: grapefruit, eggs, bacon, muffins, juice.

I think Ben and Sara were impressed with their breakfast, but it just seemed to underscore the abnormality of everything, and they hardly touched it. This may have been just as well, for in the meantime I had packed them a school lunch of such proportions that I could barely close their lunch boxes.

I had braced their teachers for Barbara's departure, and when I took Ben and Sara to school that Monday they watched all three of us vigilantly. I lingered with Ben until he'd attached himself to a classmate in the block area, and then I went to Sara's class and took dictation for half the morning as she composed a letter to her airborne mom.

The apartment I rented was pretty tight: a living room with two small bedrooms and a kitchen. But it had a wonderful location in downtown Bourne so I could walk to work, and we could all walk to the stores. The college gym was across the street, and there were tennis courts across the park and a Laundromat and Jimmy's diner a few doors down.

I had tried to devise a kind of diversionary agenda to carry the kids through those first days without their mother, but almost immediately those intentions were overwhelmed by the sheer logistics of family life. Laundry, for instance, had to be done almost every other day because there were three of us, and we didn't have many clothes. So I was always ducking over to the Laundromat a few doors down to get stuff in and out of the machines. And no matter how I tried to save money by shopping for a week's supply of food at the big supermarket on the highway, we were always running out of milk or eggs or sugar, and every evening, it seemed, we would have to hurry off to the store together.

Sara and Ben were only six and five, so of course I would drag them with me all over the place, and to do that I had to turn every errand into a kind of junket. I had to transform going to buy gas for the car into a treat just to get them moving, so I would promise them gum from the Kiwanis gum machine or a comic-book stop on the way home; or I would just try to sell them on the sheer pleasure of going for gas.

I don't know if they thought I was nuts, but they were always so positive about everything. "Oh, boy," they'd say, "we're going for gas."

It was hard to pull the same trick with my cooking. I could mix up instant mashed potatoes and bake frozen fish sticks and scramble eggs, but I didn't have the time to be fancy about it. To get them through one of my especially drab entrées I would promise them a trip to the ice cream parlor or a drive to the candy store out on the highway. And some evenings we would look in the freezer at our fish sticks and chicken pot pies, look at each other, and flee to McDonald's.

I remember that one evening I attended a faculty party where the hostess served tabouli. I thought it was terrific, and I remember saying to myself, *Hey, this is easy. I could make a pail of this stuff, and it would last all week.* So I got the recipe and went home and made this mountain of tabouli. It wound up lasting two weeks because it didn't take long for the kids to grow to hate the stuff. It became a kind of tertiary side dish as the days went by.

On school nights I would arrange all the things that we needed to start the next day: laying out clothes, packing book bags, and making sandwiches. School lunches turned into a pretty big deal because the teachers insisted that everything the kids brought in had to be natural and wholesome, and I was always getting these memos home about how hyperactivity and learning disabilities were related to diet. The teachers looked at the kids' lunch as a measure of my parenting, so there had to be cheese slices and raisins and nuts and little yogurts.

It didn't take me too long to psych all that out. I remember that once the mothers were asked to come in to help the kids prepare healthy snacks. So I came in with bags of fruit, and we all sat around making fruit salad, and I remember that Ben's classmates sweetly called out, "Thank you, Mrs. Osborne," as I departed.

The kids were pretty good about dressing themselves although how they dressed themselves could be pretty bizarre. People noticed it, I think, because they were always wearing these weird color combinations, or the wrong weight clothes for the season. I suppose I was least sensitive to Sara's clothes. She would put on these little ensembles, and I'm not sure what exactly it was she was emulating—Mag's attire, or maybe even mine—but the three of us formed a pretty frowzy trio walking down the street.

Once I was awake I was on top of things, but first the kids had to get me up in the morning. I've always had a hard time in that department, so they had to take their responsibility pretty seriously. "We'd better get Dad moving or else we're not going to get anywhere," is how they approached it, and so they would haul me out of bed and lead me to the john and leave me there to pull myself together.

Their school was only three minutes away, which was sort of a shame from my point of view because it meant that if I wanted to make up for starting late I didn't have much time to do it.

But somewhere deep down all three of us were determined to get through this, to work our way out of our misery and create a family out of what Barbara had left behind. We may have been dumped and abandoned, but we were huddled together, too, and learning that we could depend on one another.

Right from the beginning the kids were amazing the way they pitched in. I think they knew instinctively that families were vulnerable, so they stopped taking for granted the routine of family life: the interdependencies, the orderly means of getting through a day. They understood that there was a value to our continuity and that it was something we were all going to have to work on.

The kids were enrolled in an afterschool program that didn't let out until 5:30, so it was like day care, and I could put in a full day's work without worrying about them too much.

Time became precious to me: time with the kids, time at work. But the world of the single parent has no tolerances in it, and if the car broke down or one of us got sick or the dryer broke, the whole system would unravel.

We hit a period that winter when all three of us came down with influenza B. It was a killer. The kids each passed through a short but scary fever that left them shot for a few days. And then it gave me a headache of such intensity that the only way I could contain the pain was to lie perfectly still.

The problem of course was that I couldn't lie perfectly still. In addition to being a father and a teacher I was also a junior faculty member, and as such I was on a whole string of committees. It was my fault as much as the department's, I suppose, because I was always getting worked up by the bright ideas that were floating around. My old nemesis, Professor Borden, headed up an interdepartmental committee that decided that the college library, which had lost a chunk of its collection to a fire, needed beefing up. It was a pretty dreary agenda, and Borden was a master of delegation, so he put me in charge of making contact with other college libraries in the state to see if we could work out some kind of cooperative arrangement. For a couple of months I found myself driving all over Vermont, lunching with librarians.

In the meantime Ben was having what his teachers called "transition difficulty," which meant he would often cause a scene when I dropped him off at school. The teachers would assure me that just as soon as my car had disappeared from the parking lot he was always fine, but some days his pale face, contorted with sobs, seemed to follow me everywhere.

It came to a head one morning when I dropped him off with the teacher and he began to scream at the top of his lungs, as if this time he were in physical pain. The teachers in his school had a lot of developmentally based rules and procedures all laid out, and one of the cardinal ones was that if parents caved in to such demonstrations it would only make matters worse.

This particular morning I was already late for my appointment in another town, and I told Ben that I just couldn't hang around any longer. But he grabbed me around the leg, and he wouldn't let go.

The teacher tried to pry him off me and told me that it would be better if I left; I was only making it worse. I don't know who it was I heard in her voice—Barbara, probably—but nobody was going to tell me how to handle this. So I picked Ben up and I told him that it wasn't going to be any fun for him, but he could come with me if he promised to be good and quiet during my meeting.

The teacher didn't like it, but it worked. Ben was fantastic all day, sitting in the corner drawing with his crayons and listening to the give-and-take about library policies, and after that his transitions came more easily to him. It occurred to me that he must have simply needed to know that I didn't disappear into thin air—or into Israel, for that matter—when I dropped him off: that I stayed within range; that I was recoverable.

There were a few weeks when I continued to reel from influenza, and yet I still had to drive around the state making nice with librarians. One day the headache was so bad that I couldn't drive. Halfway to one of these meetings I had to pull off to the side of the road and shut my eyes, and I blew the appointment.

The next day Professor Borden called me into his office. The headache was still in full flaunt, and I must have looked ghastly: no bath, wrinkled clothes, a couple of days' beard. Borden closed the door and said he was speaking to me as a friend, but that as far as he was concerned I was going to have to make up my mind once and for all whether I was going to do this family thing or be a professional.

He made it sound as though parenting were a kick I was on, like yoga, and I went nuts. I told him he was absolutely right, and though I'd hoped not to be forced into making a choice, now that he'd put it that way my choice was simple. So I resigned from his committee.

This didn't go over too well with the department, but it was an education for me. I began to realize for the first time a little of what working mothers went through. It is as if men think that caring for a family trivializes their professional aspirations, and it's a terrible bind. I discovered that in the usual circumstances men don't understand the terrible choices working mothers are always being called upon to make between work and family.

Barbara called collect a few times during this period. She'd put Mag in a boarding school a couple of towns away, and she was as free as a bird and having a wonderful time. Every now and then in the mail would come some little Israeli keepsake for the kids: an olive-wood figure or a stack of postcards.

We talked about how I might bring the kids out for a visit, and sometimes she would talk to me about how much I would love to live out there; they needed educators, it would be great for the kids, we could all live on a kibbutz.

She used to whip up the kids with this kind of stuff, and I couldn't tell her, within their hearing, that she was crazy to think she could put everything back together on her terms.

I was doing my best, but I knew that the kids were unhappy, especially Sara. Their grief came out at odd times of the day. They would fall to pieces if something of theirs was missing, or if I were even a minute late picking them up from school.

A lot of what I remember is through the screen of my own apprehension about how they would take their mother's departure. But sometimes their eagerness and cooperativeness broke my heart. It was as though they were afraid that if they were anything less than angelic with me I might leave them too. It was strange, but under the circumstances a refusal, a complaint, even a tantrum, was enormously reassuring.

Ben tended to be less demonstrative, more complicated and oblique, always dwelling on the possibility that he was responsible in some dark way for Barbara's leaving him. I would get these reports from his teachers about fights and about the stories he would tell during their meetings: how Barbara was going to come back, and we were all going to live together happily ever after.

Sara veered back and forth between idolizing and excoriating her mother. At bedtime, when it all seemed to come down around her, she used to ask me, "How could Mommy just go like that? Isn't she going to miss me so much that she isn't going to be able to stand it?"

Neither Ben nor Sara could understand it. How could they understand it? I couldn't understand it either.

I had accepted it as my job to keep the kids thinking positively about their mother, but I felt like a doctor trying to keep Barbara's motherhood alive on a resuscitator. Whether for their sake or for mine, I used to give the kids fraudulent little bedtime pep talks about how good it was for her to be living for a while in Israel and how much she missed them and how just as soon as she could come visit them she would. I kept making excuses for her during the weeks when the flow of Israeli doodads dried up and she didn't call or answer their letters. And I did believe that Barbara cared; the problem was that she had such a hard time following through that the caring didn't always make it to the top. But the unreality of my reassurances was wearing me down.

I decided early on that I had to build a community around the kids. I was giving them everything I had, but they needed more. Sara's teacher suggested a child psychologist named Laura Mendoza, and they began to see her once a week. She gave them a chance to let off the steam they built up pitching in so cheerfully with me, and it gave me a chance to get some neutral word about how they were doing.

I also heard about a Big Brother program that had been initiated at the college, and I gave the director a call and asked if he would assign a Big Brother and a Big Sister to the kids.

"This is a very unusual request, Mr. Osborne," he said. "I'm afraid this is really meant only for underprivileged kids."

I told him I hadn't realized that there was a means test; the kids had lost a big chunk of their family, and they needed to have some good relationships with adults.

He digested that for a while, and in the end he came through. Sara's Big Sister didn't last too long, but Ben's Big Brother was this sunny kid named David who'd always wanted to have a little brother, and David latched onto the situation wonderfully. Ben thought he was a kind of superhero who'd unaccountably alighted on our tree, and the two of them, and sometimes Sara, too, would attend the college games and concerts together and ice-skate at the rink.

So the kids were in emotional intensive care those first months. We held each other together, but everything was watched. Every couple of days I would talk with the teachers, check in with Laura Mendoza, compare notes with Ben's Big Brother.

Ben's teacher was Karen Howe, one of those naturals you only come upon once or twice in school. Ben was devoted to her, and one day he invited her to dinner. It threw me to put our act on display, and I remember how we all fretted about the meal. I overcooked the roast, I think, and didn't boil the frozen peas long enough, and I couldn't figure out whether to pick the place up for a change or give her a look at how we really lived.

But she was great, and the kids were so proud to show off their stuff: the drawings they'd plastered all over the walls and the model boat we were building in the kitchen, and the coin collection we catalogued together. Karen kept reassuring me that everything was wonderful: the roast didn't matter, the mess didn't matter: if the place was messy it was also clean and warm, and the kids knew that I loved them. In the austere and desperate world of the single parent' in which I found myself, I soaked up her praise like a sponge.

The coin collection dated back to my adolescence and consisted of a lot of nickels and dimes, some of them pretty valuable. Many nights after the dishes were done Ben and Sara and I would gather on my bed and organize them into little rows, and according to our catalogues the whole collection was worth a couple of thousand dollars. In the process it acquired a lot of symbolic value and became a bond among the three of us: common stock in the continuity of the family. My bed was just an old double mattress spread out on the floor, but some nights as we huddled together on it with our nickels and dimes laid out in rows and one or another of us reporting on the triumphs and tragedies of the day, it seemed to me like a life raft on a capricious sea.

6

SUSAN

In February of 1983, Barbara and Mag returned for a couple of weeks to visit. I naturally dreaded Barbara's arrival, but I also saw it as an opportunity to show her how sharp Ben and Sara and I had become, to demonstrate to her how I thought the family should have run in the first place.

In a way this was a joke because the kids' clothes were probably on backwards, and the laundry was on the floor, but from my point of view we'd become the kind of loving, nurturing, interdependent family I'd always been shooting for. If things were a little shabby around the edges there was at least some structure to our existence and a routine upon which the kids could depend.

Barbara didn't miss any of this at all. In fact she was astounded. She even let it slip that when she'd agreed to the custody arrangement it had been with the expectation that I would eventually get worn down by the kids and beg her to take them back. She may have even thought she was going to be able to pick the kids up on that visit and take them back with her to Israel. She intimated that she would take Ben and Sara back in exchange for an adjustment in the settlement. But what she'd found instead was that I'd turned into this fierce mother hen, and I'm afraid I was out to stomp her with my goodness and efficiency as a homemaker.

We were all on our best behavior, and the visit went well, under the circumstances, even if, as Barbara put it, she sometimes thought we were "like a television sitcom, with Daddy as the audience." The kids were a little wary at first. It was hard after all those months just to visit with their mother, and I guess they figured they couldn't invest too much in Barbara again if she wasn't going to stay. At the same time they couldn't help but hope that if everything went perfectly she might change her mind about Israel and rejoin us, and I could see how in one sense her visit was setting them up for another fall. But everyone advised me that it was in the kids' best interest to see as much of their mother as possible, so I offered to let Barbara and Mag camp out in the living room.

Barbara described Israel as all milk and honey, but she wouldn't tell me much about her life there. I tried to get Mag to fill me in, but she had clammed up completely. I knew that Barbara had found work on an archaeological dig in Israel, but it didn't pay any money, and I wondered how she was going to make ends meet over the long haul; Israel was one of the most expensive places in the world to live in and Barbara had already used up most of the first of three installments of the $50,000 I'd agreed to pay her.

She did volunteer once that some guy who was in with Israeli intelligence thought she ought to join the secret service.

I said, "Great, Barbara. That would be interesting for you, plus it would be a job. You'd get a paycheck."

But I guess that wasn't the response she'd had in mind. "But it would be dangerous, Thomas," she said. "Don't you care? Aren't you concerned about what happens to me?"

That was an open question by that point, but I told her that of course I cared. I had just figured that they weren't going to be sending her undercover.

"Maybe they'll give you a desk job shredding papers or something," is the way I put it, but I could see in her eyes that I'd let her down again.

Ben's teacher, Karen Howe, met with Barbara during that visit and later reported that though Barbara had been eager to hear about the kids' successes, she absolutely refused to hear about their difficulties. I suppose it must have threatened the whole scenario she'd set up for us; things were going well for her in Israel so things had to go well for the kids too. She was in no mood to dwell on the consequences to the kids of her adventure in the Promised Land.

Part of her agenda during that trip was to persuade me to bring the kids to Israel for a visit; I would see how wonderful it was out there, and we could all go sailing together and everything would be terrific. For the time being this was out of the question, of course, because I couldn't get away from my job, and I didn't have the money. Besides, I wasn't inclined to jump through any more hoops on Barbara's account. But I don't think I ever came right out and turned her down. I may have even seemed vaguely encouraging about it, and I suppose that in her own mind she believed by the time she left that she had extracted a promise from me. When she said good-bye to Ben and Sara it was in terms of how we would all see each other next in Tel Aviv.

So Barbara and Mag returned to Israel, and the kids and I tried to pick up where we'd left off. Ben seemed to blame himself for not having managed by the sheer force of his virtue to persuade Barbara to stay. And Sara, who up to then had swung back and forth between idolizing and vilifying Barbara, felt angry and abandoned all over again.

For me the visit was a casting of the die. I hadn't realized until her visit that I too must have been harboring some faint hope that Barbara might come to her senses and return to us, but now it was obvious that she was happy with her life in Israel, thousands of miles from the kids and me. Our life together was over for good.

In those first five months I'd learned that single parenthood is a kind of barter club. I made a lot of deals with people stuck in the same straits: I'll take your boy to skating on Saturday if you pick Ben up from school on Monday; I'll take the kids trick-or-treating if you pass out candy at the door. A system of support grew up around us, and I found it was appropriate to make arrangements with people simply on the basis of common circumstances.

Even in a little town like Bourne there was a single-parent grapevine, and I would get wind of picnics, skating parties, pancake breakfasts, Saturday cartoons at the museum. Every weekend a congregation of us tempest-tossed would gather somewhere in town with our books and exam papers and Sunday papers and compare notes.

There was such a shortage of men in the Bourne area that even tenured single women tended to move away, so I got divebombed

by a lot of divorced and single women who began to see me as a
solution to their problems. Since I'd always regarded myself as more
of a problem than a solution, I was intrigued by the attention. But
at the same time I thought of myself as just another mom, and when
I bumped into a single mother in the park or a coffee shop or a faculty
party the conversation rarely advanced beyond the kids and the chal-
lenge of making do.

There never seemed to be enough time or energy to take things
any further. I began to see a little of a woman named Linda Hartley,
a professor whose husband's variation on an old cliché was to run
away with *her* secretary. But Linda also had two children, and in a
way we were more like trenchmates than anything else, cast together
by the caprice of our former spouses. We spent most of our time
commiserating.

My friends watched with alarm as I seemed to recede into a state of
nearly androgynous domesticity, and some of them did their best to
introduce me to women.

Back in September, just after Barbara and Mag had set off for
Israel, I attended the wedding of an Alden friend named Sam Kraus.
I felt like an ironic touch among the wedding guests, a recent victim
of the vicissitudes of matrimony looking on as Kathy, my buddy's
bride, came gliding down the aisle. But it had been so sweet a cer-
emony that I remember gazing fondly at one of the bridesmaids and
wondering if I would ever be fit to take the leap again.

Then in May of 1983, Sam and Kathy threw a party. It was billed
as a kind of Edwardian lawn party, with all the men dressed in white
suits and all the women wandering around in pastels sipping champagne: one of those precious annual rituals you hesitate to describe
outside your own circle, but a nice break and a chance to catch up
on far-flung friends.

Donning a dingy tan suit and leaving the kids with Aunt Jane, I
drove off to join the revels. Among the guests was the bridesmaid
upon whom I'd gazed so wistfully back in September. Kathy told me
that she was a potter from Minnesota named Susan Peale.

"Oh Jesus," I said. "Another artist."

But Kathy assured me that Susan was a big success in Minneapolis;
her plates and pots sold in all the major outlets in the Twin Cities

area, and her business often brought her east to deliver her wares to stores and galleries in Boston and New York.

Susan was a tall, blonde, wiry woman in her early thirties, and from the beginning of the festivities she seemed to exercise a kind of magnetic pull. Her reticence, in almost contradictory combination with her large blue eyes and generous mouth, intrigued me. Whenever I looked her way, she seemed to be the calm in the eye of the storm and returned my gaze evenly, with an almost unsettling intelligence and composure. I have always been given to reading too much into a woman's face, but just beneath her reserve I saw substance and generosity, and a solid center of gravity.

I kept balking and telling myself, "Forget it, Osborne. This woman is too healthy for you." But I couldn't take my eyes off her and arranged for a group of us to have dinner that evening at a local restaurant called Pietro's.

As we waited outside for a table, it began to rain, and Susan and I found ourselves huddled together under a canopy next door. I guess my inquiries and my fond gazes during the party had unsettled the both of us, and we were tongue-tied.

But as we took a few futile stabs at small talk, an acquaintance of mine happened to duck by, a professor in another department at Bourne whose daughter was in Ben's class. He spoke to me briefly, and then as he bade us farewell he turned to Susan and said, "You should be very proud, Mrs. Osborne. Your kids are really beautiful."

I guess Susan didn't want to embarrass him, so she said, "Yes, thank you. They're lovely."

This broke the ice somewhat, and the next morning when I brought Ben and Sara by to meet her the standing joke was, "Well, Susan, here are your kids."

I realized that despite the auspiciousness of my colleague's remark I had not made much of an impression on Susan the evening before. Trying to show off my erudition I got entangled in a long exchange with Sam about immigration. My intellectual exhibitionism had worked with Barbara when I'd first met her, but listening to Sam and me talk for two hours straight evidently wasn't Susan's idea of a good time.

By evening's end I was afraid that I had blown it completely with

Susan Peale. But I was determined to take at least one more swing at the ball, and when Susan mentioned that she would be driving east in early July, I got her to promise to stop off in Alden, where the kids and I would be vacationing with the Osborne clan.

The kids had tolerated my harmless relationship with Linda Hartley, but they sensed that I was working up to something serious over Susan. My colleague's remark to Susan—"Here are your children"—had been a tip-off, and I kept mentioning her in conversation when people dropped by, as though some great affair were already under way.

Sara seemed at first to be the most encouraging, teasing me and egging me on when the subject arose. She was hard to read, but I think she missed her mother more than any of us and yet at the same time had the fewest illusions about a reconciliation.

But Ben had never really given up hope and was therefore more complicated about Susan. I couldn't tell if he wanted to prevent my precluding Barbara's return or to prevent my bringing another Barbara into a domestic arrangement with which he'd finally come to terms.

"Dad, I've got to talk to you," he'd say, taking me aside. "Do you really *like* this woman? I mean, what are you *doing* with her?"

"It's going to be okay, Ben," I'd try to tell him. "She's just somebody nice I'm glad I've met."

But Ben and Sara knew that Susan already loomed larger than that, and I tried to orchestrate in advance her visit to the Peaceable Kingdom. Out of the reassurance I derived from the fact that Susan was the best friend of my own best friend's wife, and from my own anguished intuition about her, I was prepared to take our relationship as far as it would go.

It turned out that Susan was in the same frame of mind. As far back as the wedding in September she had evidently known about my interest in her, and Kathy, in turn, was pushing her forward. Things had even progressed to the point where her friends in Minnesota had taken to telling her that she was going to Alden to meet her husband. For her part Susan wasn't at all sure she wanted to get involved with a man who was broke, divorced, and saddled with two small children. But even though she had never married, family was important to her and, according to Kathy, she was looking for a change.

That spring I kept veering between my pride in how well the kids and I were doing and this heartbreaking sense that somewhere, maybe even back before Ben and Sara were born, I had let them down. I still appreciated the positive side of my situation, which was that my life had acquired a touchstone, and whether that touchstone was assembling a couple of peanut butter and jelly sandwiches or getting the kids to school or doing the laundry or tucking them into bed, I had learned that my family had to come first in my life. For all our pain the three of us had entered a time of definition and abiding and taking care. But even though the kids and I were holding ourselves together all right, we weren't exactly thriving.

So I decided to leave Bourne and return to the clan in Alden. It had been made plain to me that without a Ph.D. my career at Bourne College was dead-ended. I applied and was accepted into a doctoral program at Brandeis, on the condition that I spend August taking an intensive refresher course in statistics.

My plan had been to keep the kids with Aunt Jane in Alden while I took the course, but in June Barbara announced that she and Mag would return that summer to visit Ben and Sara and pick up her final check. By this time the civility we'd cultivated in February had worn off. She was angry that I hadn't brought the kids to Israel to visit her, and I was still damned if I was going to bankroll some accommodation to her abandonment of Ben and Sara.

We managed, somehow, to make a deal. Barbara wanted to send Mag ahead of her, so I agreed to take her on in Alden for the month of July. I also agreed that Barbara could have my apartment and my car, and could visit with the kids for three weeks in August, just so long as she arrived in Bourne by August 2nd, in time for me to begin my statistics course in Boston.

Mag arrived in early July, and first thing one Saturday morning the four of us drove down to Alden together. Mag was still being squirrelly with me, but she seemed glad to be back with her brother and sister.

I guess I didn't realize how exhausted I was until I pulled into Uncle Henry's driveway that noon. As soon as my niece took the kids under her wing, and I could finally let my guard down, I passed out in a deck chair on Uncle Henry's terrace and didn't move until supper.

I spent a week sailing and fishing and swimming with the kids, reading from the frayed family copies of Kipling and Twain to Sara, and building models with Ben in the boathouse. By the time Susan arrived on the 11th I was restored.

She looked radiant as she stepped out of her car in the cottage drive, and she greeted the kids with such instinctive respect—kneeling down and speaking quietly to them, without a trace of irony—that for the first few hours they would hardly let her out of their sight. I found that on my own turf I wasn't at such a loss for conversation, and we spent the day touring the Peaceable Kingdom together, strolling along the beach and briefly setting sail around Alden harbor.

The kids were at their best those four days: bright and affectionate and enthusiastic as they darted from house to house with their games and projects. My niece held down the fort with them at mealtime so that Susan and I could go off to eat at local restaurants and compare notes on the vicissitudes of life. I had determined that I would not lean on the subject of my divorce as my conversational crutch, but it spilled out one way or another. For her part Susan told me about a couple of long-term relationships she'd had, and it was clear that she was weary of having them come to nothing.

I could hardly believe that a woman of her grace and gravity could have been interested in someone as battle-scarred as I, but I derived such sustenance from her that I took it as almost a validation of my mental health. In those four days I realized for the first time that I'd come a little distance since Barbara Kaye.

In short, I fell in love with Susan Peale, and couldn't bear to see her go. Before those four days came to a close I made her promise to visit us in Bourne at the end of the month, on her way back to Minnesota. However absurd it may sound from this remove, I knew as I kissed her good-bye that I was going to marry her.

When I checked out this proposition with the kids Mag seemed to take it in stride. Sara seemed ecstatic at first; there'd be another female around the house, she'd have a mother again.

But Ben's reaction was to shake his head, as if in all my years with Barbara I hadn't learned a thing.

"Oh man," he said gravely, "this is going to piss Mom off so much."

7

THE COINS

On the 24th of July, 1983, Susan Peale came to Bourne. I was afraid that beyond the idyllic premises of the Peaceable Kingdom the whole affair might collapse around us. There was no idealizing the apartment, and the kids and I still looked like ruffled ducks out on the streets of Bourne. But we seemed to confirm Susan's intuition that for all our dishevelment we were standing by each other. She delighted in the kids' show-and-tell and even took part in our evening ritual with the coin collection, cataloguing our nickels and dimes in Ben's tattered looseleaf notebook.

After four more splendid days Susan Peale agreed to marry me. I slipped an engagement ring on her finger as we sat under a sycamore on the town green and the kids splashed about in the fountain. But we both hedged our bets a little. Despite the ring we tried to regard our engagement as unofficial until I'd met her parents. She decided not to mention it to her friends for fear they would all tell her she would have to be crazy to marry someone she'd just met. In addition, we decided not to marry right away but to ease everyone toward it; she would move with us to Alden in September, and we would see how things worked out. But neither of us was really questioning the rightness of our feeling for each other and the confluence of events that had drawn us together.

Shortly after Susan left for Minnesota I called Barbara to see if she'd made reservations yet for her trip in August.

Barbara had been in even less frequent contact than usual with the kids, but from what little Mag had let slip I learned that she was not exactly flourishing in Israel. Barbara never had found work and her money had nearly run out again: she'd spent almost all of the $16,666 I'd given her since the settlement, which left her with only the remaining two payments of $16,666 to see her through.

The psychologist we'd visited once told me that Barbara's notion of divorce was for me to remain next door: accessible, supportive, a kind of husband-on-demand. All the other pieces on the checkerboard would stay in place except her; she would be free to collect her alimony and travel the world and be Jewish and do whatever she wanted.

So, like Ben, I expected the news of my engagement to go off like a bombshell, and when she called I toyed for a moment with not telling Barbara about Susan at all. But I figured it would be fairer to everyone if I gave her a chance to come to terms with it now, before she reached the kids.

"So, Barbara," I said, bracing myself. "I've got a little news."

"News, Thomas?" she said. "What news is that?"

"I've met someone," I told her, "and we're getting married."

I don't know what I was expecting: histrionics, maybe; anger, certainly. But there was only the briefest pause.

"Well, Thomas," she said. *"Mazel tov."*

I began to think that maybe Ben and the psychologist were wrong about Barbara. Maybe my marrying Susan suited her perfectly, freed her up even more for her adventures.

But as August 2nd approached, Barbara still hadn't made any reservations. I kept calling and asking her when she was coming. "Barbara, you've got to be here in time," I told her. "If we're going to follow this plan so you can visit with the kids, you're going to have to get here in time for me to start my class."

She said, "Well, I can't really finalize my arrangements yet, Thomas."

"What do you mean you can't finalize your arrangements?" I said. "I'm working. I'm going to school. I've got to do things with some precision. And you sit over there and don't do anything, and you tell me you can't finalize your arrangements?"

The kids were naturally excited that their mother was coming back, and on August 2nd I prepared to pass the baton and drive down to Boston. But by eight o'clock that evening there was still no sign of Barbara.

I began to call everyone I could think of. There was no answer at her number in Israel, and neither her mother nor any of her stateside friends knew where she was. I had only one more card up my sleeve if she didn't show—my poor mother—and on the afternoon of the 3rd I finally asked her to come up and hold the fort until Barbara arrived.

So my mother threw her things together and came huffing and puffing up from Florida. The kids were perplexed by the change of plan, and I drove off to Boston in a cloud of gloom. I believed that I'd tried to be generous and accommodating so Barbara could visit the kids, and now here she was jerking me around all the way from Israel.

When I called my mother on the 4th there was still no sign of Barbara. Nobody'd heard from her. Nobody knew where she was. My mother assured me that everything was all right; she and the children were doing fine. But then another day passed and another, and it wasn't until the following Tuesday, August 9th, that Barbara appeared at the door, in a froth of righteous indignation.

What was my mother doing there? she demanded to know. Why wasn't I there to greet her? Here she'd come all this way, and I wasn't even there to let her into the apartment.

My mother was so stunned that she could only watch as Barbara hurried the kids out the door.

The course I was in was one of those eight-hour-a-day jobs where if you missed a couple of days you were out. But I skipped a day and drove the three hours back to Bourne, thinking, *Goddamn it. This is* my *life. When is she going to clear out of it?*

By the time I got there the kids had been gone for six hours, and my mother was in a state. I told her it wasn't her fault—there was nothing she could have done. Everything was going to be fine.

But as I drove from motel to motel, it occurred to me for the first time in all this that Barbara might take the children.

By eight o'clock that night I had covered every inn and motel in the area, checked at the bus station, peered through every restaurant window. I was about to return to the apartment to confer with my mother when I finally caught sight of Barbara and the kids strolling along the sidewalk in the dark.

The kids waved at me cheerfully as I screeched to a halt beside them, and Barbara stiffened to attention, jutting her chin.

"Goddamn it, Barbara," I said, taking her aside. "What the hell is going on? What are you doing out here?"

"It's nice to see you too, Thomas," she said with a sigh. "I am taking the children for a walk."

"Taking the children for a walk? Look," I said. "I told you I needed you here on the second. That was the deal. Where the hell *were* you?"

"Well, it didn't work out that way, did it, Thomas?" Barbara said, smiling slightly at Mag. "You think I was late on purpose? You think I meant to ruin your precious plans?"

"Then what happened? Where were you?"

"What difference does that make? What's the point of going over this now, Thomas? Have you stopped to think how *I* felt when I got to the apartment, and *you* weren't there?"

"Well, what did you expect? I told you I had to start this course."

"And everything has to revolve around you? Is that it? You just farm out our children because of some silly course?"

I gaped at her a moment, and then Susan's face appeared before me, and I felt very calm.

"You're not going to buffalo me anymore, Barbara," I said as softly and as steadily as I could. "You screwed up. Don't screw up again."

"Well," said Barbara. "*There's* a fine welcome home."

All the old fear came back as I installed Barbara in my apartment and drove my mother to the airport. I felt as though this claw had risen up out of my past to drag us all back. I kept thinking, *What if she does mean to steal my kids away?* But I couldn't see how she could do it. I couldn't imagine Barbara putting all the pieces together.

Before I drove back to Boston we met in my car outside the apartment. I told her that things were going to have to be different. "Listen, Barbara," I said, "the kids are used to a routine now."

"Oh really, Thomas?" she said, busying herself with something in her shoulder bag. "With women traipsing in and out of your apartment all the time?"

"What are you talking about?"

"You know what I'm talking about," she said. "The kids have told me plenty."

"Look, Barbara," I said, trying not to rise to the bait. "I don't know what you're talking about. What I do know is that they've become used to regular meals, to getting picked up on time, to getting dropped off on schedule, to going to bed by eight. They've got to have some order, Barbara. They've got to have some security."

"I think I know how to raise my own children, Thomas," Barbara said, folding her arms. "I am their mother, you know."

I tried to rein myself in again, but staring back at her now in the dim light I couldn't do it. "What the hell do you mean, you're their mother? You think you can come traipsing back every ten months and pass yourself off as their mother?"

"What do you mean, *Pass myself off?*" she said. "You can't talk to me like that!"

"I can talk to you any goddamn way I please, Barbara. You left us all behind. You left me holding the bag. What kind of mother," I asked, and I was shouting now, "ditches her own children?"

She looked at me then, and for a moment I thought I'd finally poked through all the fantasy she'd built up around herself. But just as instantaneously the look of recognition vanished, and she swung back her arm and slapped me across the face.

The blow snapped my head to the side, but I tried not to flinch. I slowly faced her again, gripping the steering wheel with both hands. "You can slap people around all you like," I told her as she fumbled with the door handle. "But it won't change the truth."

Nevertheless, I realized as she slammed the door behind her that in the name of having it out in that poisonous exchange I had dangerously upped the ante.

My jaw still stung as I pored over my books that night. During the next few days I kept calling the kids to make sure they were all right, and whenever there was no answer or even when the line was busy I would start to convince myself that she'd run off with them and I would pace around the room. When I finally did get through to Ben and Sara I rejoiced in the sound of their voices; they were fine, they were safe, they were home. We were all going to make the future work.

One weekend Herman Stack, my old boss in the Vaughn Islands, showed up in Bourne, and I drove up to meet him and his new wife.

It was a miserable visit. By the time I got to Bourne Barbara had already given Herman an earful. He took me aside and put one avuncular arm over my shoulder and suggested that maybe I was being just a little too rough on Barbara; she was sensitive, after all, and, besides, she *was* the mother of my children.

I couldn't answer him. How could I explain everything that had happened between Barbara and me since I'd seen him last? If he really believed that I'd been too hard on Barbara then he was too far off base for me to enlighten. He was into his second marriage himself; where did he get off handing out advice? So as we sat eating our little luncheon I wrote off Herman Stack.

Barbara kept mentioning a diamond merchant named Marcus she'd met back in Israel, as if this Marcus were someone important to her, but I wouldn't pick up on it, perhaps because I sensed how much she hoped I would.

But she'd saved the main event for the dessert course, announcing as she served up berries and cream that she had decided not to go back to Israel after all, but to move to Alden to be near her children.

So there it was again. I was never going to be free of her. First Barbara had menaced my education, and now she was menacing my life with Susan. Barbara had thrown me out and abandoned the kids, and now she was going to hang around and keep doing all the nasty things she'd always done forever.

So I dragged myself off to see Uncle Henry. At the time his own life was backing up on him too. A real-estate conglomerate was gunning for the family firm and flashing a lot of money around at his directors, and for all his rage at the conference table Uncle Henry was losing ground.

But he rallied for my sake and managed to frame my situation into manageable proportions. Vigilance was going to be called for, and no more of my whining. The first order of business was to call Bowles, my divorce lawyer, and nail down a new visitation agreement.

So Bowles approached Fletcher, Barbara's attorney, and arranged for an arbitration meeting at the end of the month. In the meantime Barbara asked that I have my trust officer cut her a second check for $16,666, and on Bowles's advice I agreed, just to keep my own nose clean.

The statistics course was murder. I studied during the evenings, trying to approach all those alien digits and columns and formulae as intriguing puzzles and brainteasers. By the end of the summer I had managed to pass the course. I drove off to Minneapolis to pick up Susan and meet her folks.

They may have been a little dubious about me at first, but I think Susan must have derived some of her innate poise from the trust they obviously reposed in her. They were pleased that I would be so old-fashioned as to ask her father for his daughter's hand and they seemed to need even less reassurance than Susan did when I told them about Barbara's plan to move to Alden.

Despite all my declarations of trust that everything was to going to work out, I think I was probably the least confident of all of us. But I was much stronger when I was with Susan, and I decided that Barbara was not going to rob us of our happiness.

Jutting our jaws, Susan and I made the journey back to New Hampshire to pick up the kids. By the time we reached Bourne on Sunday afternoon, August 28th, we were weary but full of resolution. Whatever it took, we were going to make everything work.

I parked the car by the curb and dashed upstairs to the apartment. "Sara, Ben," I said, knocking on the door. "It's Dad."

I waited a moment and knocked again as Susan caught up with me on the landing.

"Aren't they home?" she asked.

"Damn it," I said, digging for my keys. "I don't know."

I unlocked the door, and we walked in to find the place immaculate—cleaner than I'd ever seen it. But there was no sign of the kids.

"Oh Jesus," I started to say, standing in the middle of the living room. "She's taken them."

But almost immediately the phone rang.

"Hello, Thomas."

"Barbara?"

"Yes, Thomas. I'm in Boston."

"Barbara, where are the kids?"

"Oh, I'm sorry, Thomas," she said. "Yesterday they decided they wanted to see the aquarium, and it got so late we decided to spend the weekend here."

"Where's 'here'?"

"At some friends'," she said quickly. "But the reason I'm calling, Thomas, is I wonder if it would be all right if I held onto them until tomorrow. I'd like to spend tonight up here and then bring them in to the arbitration."

I paused to catch my breath. "Are they all right?"

"Yes, of course they're all right. Oh, and Thomas," said Barbara. "The settlement check hadn't come when I left."

I stooped down and shuffled through the mail scattered by the door. "It's here," I said, finding an envelope from Waters & Dunne, my trustees.

"Could you do me a favor?" Barbara asked. "Could you have Federal Express or something get the check to me right away?"

I frowned and watched as Susan entered the children's room.

"I'll just give it to you on Monday."

"Well," said Barbara. "I would really prefer it if you could get it to me right now."

"Barbara," I said. "It's Sunday. What difference is one day going to make?"

There was a silence on the other end, and then I could hear Barbara sigh. "All right, Thomas. If that's the way you want it. Give it to me on Monday," and she hung up the phone.

"Why does she need the check now?" I asked as Susan appeared in the doorway of the children's room.

"Thomas," she said tentatively. "I think you'd better look in here."

The children's room was empty. All of Ben and Sara's toys, all their books, even their sheets and blankets, were gone.

I was certain that Barbara had planned a run with the children. But what kind of run? I assumed that without my signature as custodial parent she couldn't obtain passports for the children, so where could she take them? Back to the Vaughn Islands? To her mother in Colorado?

Or had she simply intended to take the kids for a week or so, just to throw her weight around, just to teach me a lesson for taking up with Susan and throwing all her plans into disarray?

By late that evening Susan and I had convinced ourselves that Barbara must have miscalculated and that so long as I had her check I was in control.

8

THE VISITATION

The next morning Barbara arrived on time and cordially handed Ben and Sara over to Susan. Sara greeted us effusively, but Ben looked a little sheepish, as if he were harboring a secret.

This was Susan's first meeting with Barbara, and she was impressed by how calm Barbara was, and how civil, after everything I'd said about her. Ben and Sara and Mag stumbled under boxes and bundles of toys and linens, and Susan helped them carry everything downstairs to the car. Susan remembers feeling like a governess, waiting with them in a nearby park as Barbara and I and our respective attorneys filed into the arbitrator's office.

Once we'd all taken our seats, Barbara made her announcement official: she and Mag were not returning to Israel; they were moving to Alden to be near Ben and Sara.

The arbitrator, a plump, phlegmatic man named Dinsmore, looked pleased and said he thought she was making a good decision. But as they sat there grinning at each other I exploded.

"All right, Barbara," I said, "if that's what you're going to do— if you're just going to hang around and haunt me and Susan and the kids, then we can't carry on like this. You can't just traipse off with the children anytime you like. You can't keep tugging them back and forth. You can't screw up our lives," I said, gripping the arms of my chair now and leaning toward her.

"Take it easy, Tom," said Bowles, nudging my arm.

Dinsmore frowned at me. "Tom, I don't feel that you're taking this in the right spirit. Mrs. Osborne has—"

But Barbara calmly raised her hand for silence, smiling at Dinsmore. "I don't intend to do anything to complicate his life, Mr. Dinsmore," she said. "I intend to lead my own life. I'm not going to center everything around Thomas and his *Susan*."

I narrowed my eyes at Barbara but sat back, trying to compose myself. "Okay, Barbara," I said. "We'll make it work. It'll be good for the kids to have you nearby," I said. "But we've got to get this nailed down."

Fletcher broke in, opening his briefcase on the floor beside him. "I think we all recognize the need for that, Tom," he said. "And I think you'll be pleased with Barbara's decision in that regard."

And in fact there was nothing for Dinsmore to arbitrate. Barbara had agreed to everything I'd asked for; she would have Ben and Sara only every other weekend from Friday until Tuesday, and on Tuesday afternoons every other week.

I had won, after a fashion, but when Barbara and I left Dinsmore's office, and Susan caught sight of us coming up the street, she presumed I'd lost, because I seemed so abstracted as I handed Barbara her final check, and Barbara was all smiles.

As we packed the next day for the move to Alden, I tried to concentrate on the future. Barbara had blown fog across the landscape, but maybe it was egocentric of me to think she was really out to ruin me. Maybe, as Susan gently suggested, I was overreacting. If Susan could handle it, why couldn't I? And how could I begrudge Ben and Sara their mother's proximity? Maybe Alden would be a renewal for everyone.

The house I'd rented was my cousin Tod's small, shingled cottage across the stone drive from Uncle Henry's house. A long narrow strip of yard ran through a clump of woods from the back door all the way down to the shore. The cottage had begun as a one-bedroom, L-shaped affair with a living room at one end and a small dining room, bedroom, kitchen, and bath jammed into the other. But Tod had added two more bedrooms beyond the kitchen—large, airy rooms with sliding glass doors opening out onto views of the shore—and the large garage was heated and light enough to accommodate Susan's studio.

On Saturday, September 3rd, Ben, Sara, Susan, and I arrived at the house with a trailer in tow, and all ran out to the shore to watch the buffleheads bobbing in the flashing silver water. I remember it was a cool, breezy day, and great clouds drifted overhead as we let ourselves into the unlocked house.

I embraced Susan in the kitchen as Ben and Sara laid claim to their sunlit rooms, and it did seem that night as Susan and I lined the kitchen shelves with newspaper, as Sara set out her stuffed animals and Ben unpacked his paints, that we had finally found a sanctuary in the Peaceable Kingdom.

I hadn't heard from Barbara since the arbitration, but on September 5th she called to announce that she and Mag had moved temporarily into a cabin at the Dunrollin Motel in Hammond, just across the Alden line. There was no phone in the cottage, she explained, so she would be calling from a pay phone at Augie's Service Station across the highway.

I remembered the Dunrollin as a seedy little collection of cabins on Route 11 that served a transient clientele of adulterers, week-enders, and fraternity revelers. There was an old tile pool edged with cedars, a cracked shuffleboard court, and a rowboat planter filled with marigolds under the sign by the road.

As Barbara unpacked at the Dunrollin, I picked up Mag and brought her home to swim with the kids off the cobble beach. She was so pleased to be with Ben and Sara again and beamed when they came bursting up to the car to greet her. But she was taciturn around Susan and me, and when Susan called everyone back to the house and offered them cups of hot cider, Mag declined and roosted on a kitchen stool, skinny and shivering in her towel, watching her siblings drink like a mute and vigilant mother bird.

I was troubled by the thought of Mag with her mother in their seedy little motel cottage, walking along Route 11 for meals at the Frosty Freeze. But when I dropped Mag off, Barbara assured me that it was only temporary; she was looking for a house to rent and had a lead on a job somewhere in the area. So, for the time being, all I could do was hope Mag would be all right.

One evening as we were unpacking some boxes we'd hauled down from Bourne, Ben took me aside and peered up at me the way he did whenever he had something important to impart: with his lips set straight and his small brow furrowed. He'd seemed troubled by something ever since I'd picked him up, and I was afraid it was Susan.

"Dad," he said once we were alone. "I've got something I've got to tell you, and it's going to make you mad."

"At you?"

"Well," he said, turning and glancing at me sidelong. "I don't know. It wasn't my idea, Dad. But Dad?"

"What is it, Ben?"

"Dad," he said, "Mom sold some of our coins."

"She *what*?"

"Oh boy," said Ben. "I knew I shouldn't have told you," and he began to cry.

Sara suddenly became angry at him. "Oh *Ben*," she said. "Mommy *told* us not to tell."

But then she broke down as well and told me that a few days after my lunch with her and Herman Stack Barbara had sold the coins to a dealer for $150.

So not only had Barbara sold our coins, but she'd made it so that Ben and Sara had come to regard themselves as accomplices in her little crime. I didn't need a psychiatrist to tell me that it wasn't the $150 Barbara had been gunning for but the bond that had developed between the kids and me.

I called Bowles and had him locate the dealer for me, an elderly man named Huff who remembered Barbara coming into his Burlington shop with Ben and Sara on August 23rd. Barbara had told him that she'd bought the coins from a friend in New Jersey and had been keeping them in a safe deposit box in Hanover. He claimed not to remember what the coins were, but he bought them from her for $152, to be exact, and promptly sold them to a collector.

"What's the difference?" Barbara wanted to know when I confronted her on the phone. "They weren't worth anything anyway."

"Weren't worth anything? They were worth several thousand dollars. They were a bond between Ben and Sara and me. And you go off with the kids to some dealer and sell them for a hundred and fifty-two dollars?"

"Well, it's not *stealing*, Thomas," she said. "Remember—I gave you some of those coins myself."

What was I going to do? Call the cops on her?

"No, Tom," said Uncle Henry, "just add it to the dossier. Look, damn it," he told me. "The worst she can do is take the kids, and if she takes the kids we'll find them, and then you'll finally have the leverage to hold onto them."

His confidence that whatever happened we would prevail became like a touchstone, so that every time Susan and I began to despair I would say to her, "But it's just like Uncle Henry says. We're going to come out of this, and all the forces of justice that have always seemed so vague before will come out on our side."

To give us a head start in that direction, Uncle Henry advised me to drop Bowles and call in some high-powered legal guns from the family's firm of Partridge Osborne and Lanier. The Osborne had been my great-great Uncle Louis, a hero of the battle of Shiloh who, by the time of his death in 1926, had built the firm into one of the most prestigious in Boston: mediator, guardian and trustee to the Brahminical caste of Beacon Hill. I'd been content with Bowles's legal services, but Uncle Henry convinced me that if Barbara were up to something I was going to need the full power and influence of a major law firm. I made an appointment with Peter Hill, one of the firm's domestic relations specialists, in his office overlooking the Common.

A tall, tow-headed, courtly man in his middle forties, Hill showed me to a deep leather armchair in his office.

"Now then, Tom," he said, selecting a pipe from the windowsill and digging into his vest pocket. "What can I do for you?"

I handed him the documents from the divorce and arbitration, along with a letter Bowles had obtained from the coin dealer. Hill leaned forward and reviewed them as I stared around the office: a mahogany vault containing a collection of pipes in a glass case, two walls lined with law books, and a vast and tidy desk with a green leather top.

"Seems to be in order," Hill said finally, leaning back again and sniffing slightly.

I told Hill about Barbara's jaunt to Boston, her visit to the pawn-broker, her oblique threats about her boyfriend Marcus and Israeli Intelligence and all the rest of it, as Hill leaned back with a creaking noise and packed his pipe from a Florentine pouch.

She had the money, I told him, but she wasn't settling down. She wasn't looking for a job. She hadn't bought herself a car. Mag wasn't enrolled in school. I couldn't figure out if I was paranoid or if she was planning something, and it was driving me nuts.

When I was done Hill puffed on his pipe for a moment, making faint chirping noises as he stared across the room.

"Offhand," he said finally, "I think you're right to keep me posted." I asked if there was anything he could do to get the coins back.

He sniffed and leaned far back in his chair. He had to say it was doubtful, but it was worth having some documentation in case she gave me any further trouble.

What kind of trouble?

Hill ran a hand over his stomach, smoothing his tie. That was hard to say, but from what I was telling him it looked as though there might be a potential for some visitation problems here.

"Now I don't think you should be too alarmed at this point, Tom," he said finally, rising from his desk. "But I do want you to know that I'm available if you need me."

So I shook hands with Hill and took my leave. Waiting for the elevator I gazed along the shelves of law books in the firm's library and stared a moment at great-great Uncle Louis himself in the found-ers' gallery, exuding confidence from several dozen square feet of oil and canvas.

The kids were to start at the Alden School on Tuesday, but I made an appointment ahead of time with the principal, a Mr. Lepke, to fill him in on my children's circumstances.

The school had been newly renovated that summer and Lepke showed me around with pride, pointing out all the new facilities he'd managed to exact from the local school board: audiovisual equip-ment, a bright new library, a skylit art room.

I met Ben and Sara's teachers and liked them on sight; they seemed to be fresh to the system and eager to know all about Ben and Sara.

But my main concern as we sat in one of the classrooms was that Lepke and the staff keep a special eye out for my children.

"We keep what you call a special eye out for all our kids, Mr. Osborne," Lepke told me expansively.

"I don't mean to suggest you don't," I said. "But you see, their mother's been acting erratically lately, Mr. Lepke, and I'd appreciate it if you could just be sure that the kids don't leave the school with her without my permission."

"You mean there's a custody problem?" Lepke asked.

"Yes, you see—"

"Well, Mr. Osborne," he said, rising to his feet. "I'm afraid I can't do much without a court order."

"I'm not asking you to be a cop, Mr. Lepke. I just want you to keep an eye on them. Give me a call when she contacts you. That sort of thing."

"Well," said Lepke. "I can't take any responsibility, but I'll see what I can do."

On Tuesday I drove Ben and Sara to school and waited with them for the morning bell. They already knew a couple of kids from the neighborhood, including a serious boy named Geoffrey who approached them immediately and was full of solemn advice about how to get along. The first day of school always gave me an empty feeling in the pit of my stomach, but Ben and Sara were cheerful and seemed to melt comfortably into the flow of children as everyone filed through the door.

On Thursday the 8th I had to go into Waltham to register for my classes. By this time I'd shored myself up a little, and I was thinking that if my fear was really just residual anger at Barbara I'd better put it behind me or nothing was going to work. And it was in that spirit that I agreed to let Barbara hitch a ride with me into the city. She still lacked not only a car but an American driver's license and needed to retrieve some suitcases she'd left at a hotel in Boston.

So I picked her up at the Dunrollin, and she was pleasant enough for several miles, chatting about this and that. She began to quote from a book she'd been reading whose thesis was that war was the main driving force of culture and that it was only through conflict that human beings were challenged into progressing.

Barbara always advocated whatever she was reading, and in the old days I might have accepted it as transitory and kept my mouth shut. But I'd seen this before, back during the divorce. She was rationalizing something apocalyptic, and it galled me as I glanced at her sitting primly on the seat beside me. What was she doing here? What was she up to? Why didn't she leave me alone?

"So what are you saying, Barbara?" I said. "That you can't make a frost-free refrigerator without wiping out a hundred thousand people?"

Barbara crossed her arms and glared straight ahead, chewing on the inside of her cheek as we drove up to her hotel.

"You know, Thomas," she said finally as we pulled up to the door. "I've got you figured out."

"Good. Finally," I said. "You've got me figured out."

"That's right," said Barbara, climbing out of the car. "You would like to be Yoda," she said, "but you're really Darth Vader."

The visitation agreement called for the kids to stay with Barbara from Friday through Tuesday, so I supplied her with a note to the principal, and we arranged for her to pick them up after school on Friday afternoon.

Since Barbara still had no car they all had to walk along Route 11 for meals at the Frosty Freeze and games of miniature golf down by the drive-in. All through that weekend I kept inventing little excuses for dropping by: delivering a stuffed animal, picking up laundry, anything I could think of just to be sure Ben and Sara were all right. I even checked the bus schedule and drove by the station whenever a bus was due to depart.

In the meantime Susan was planning Ben and Sara's sixth and seventh respective birthdays the following Wednesday. We invited all of their new classmates, and Susan and the kids drew up plans for the cakes. There would be games on the lawn, and as a finale the kids and I would launch some rocket models we'd constructed out in the boathouse.

My last drop-in visit to the Dunrollin was about two o'clock on

Sunday afternoon, September 12th. It was a hot, still day, and I found Barbara and the kids eating take-out burgers by the pool. Barbara said she had something to talk about and followed me to the cabin as I walked over to leave a stuffed bear on Sara's bed.

The cabin was a cramped little room with faded floral wallpaper and a couple of metal frame beds, an old black-and-white television, a TV tray, and a warped bureau painted blue.

"Thomas," she said as I set down the bear. "I want to come to the kids' birthday."

I ran my hand over my brow. Susan and I had prepared ourselves for this and come to the same conclusion: she was their mother; of course she could come to their birthday party.

"All right, Barbara."

"I think it would be better for the kids if I were there."

"I said, 'All right, Barbara.' That's fine."

It wasn't fine, of course, and I thought of Susan then, shopping for pans for the birthday cake.

"And I would like to bring someone with me," Barbara said as we stepped back outside.

Ben was now treading water in the deep end, and I called out to him. "You know better than that, Ben," I told him. "Don't go in without a grownup around."

"Sorry, Dad."

"Will that be all right?" Barbara asked, crossing her arms as I reached the pool.

"Will what be all right?"

"If I bring a guest."

I stooped down and hauled Ben out of the water. "Yes," I said. "You can bring a guest."

"Well, don't you want to know who it is?"

"It doesn't matter," I said, wrapping a towel around Ben.

"It doesn't matter?" asked Barbara. "It doesn't matter who comes to your children's birthday party?"

"No," I said. "I just mean you can bring whoever you want to bring."

"Well, it's Marcus," she said, raising her chin slightly. "I'm bringing Marcus."

"Fine," I said. "Bring Marcus."

Suddenly Barbara stormed past me. "Who needs *you*, anyway?" she said, snatching up burger wrappers from around the pool. Sara crouched down slightly and pretended to interest herself in Mag's magazine as Ben hurried back to the cabin.

"Take it easy, Barbara," I said, glancing toward the Dunrollin office, where Mrs. Garafolo now appeared in the window.

"I'll take it easy," she said. "I'll take it easy. Who needs you? I don't need you. I have *Marcus*. *Marcus* is going to take care of me."

"You be good," I told Sara, giving her a kiss as I climbed into my car.

"I will, Daddy," she said.

"And remember this," Barbara called after me, keeping pace as I backed out the driveway. "Marcus is going to take care of you too, Thomas. Marcus is going to take care of *you!*"

As I drove past the cabin Ben appeared in the doorway, waving to me in the dwindling light.

9

25 BRISBY STREET

On Monday I drove to Brandeis for my first class in my doctoral program: an evening seminar on immigration trends taught by a well-scrubbed young man named Coates. He looked to me like just a kid, but if he was just a kid my fellow classmates must have been newborns: fresh-faced, sneakered, with gag stickers already stuck to their textbook covers.

I felt dull and overgrown, like a held-back teenager in a fifth-grade class. I looked across at the others jotting their notes in tabulated notebooks and then gazed out the window at the dusk light of the campus, thinking of the kids, hoping Barbara was getting them to bed on time.

"Excuse me," someone was saying from the front of the room.

I looked forward. Coates was glaring at me. "Can I have *everyone's* attention?" he wanted to know.

"Yes," I said as the others turned toward me. "Sorry."

Coates pushed his glasses up his nose and resumed his lecture. As I bent over my notebook I hoped Ben and Sara had had better luck in school that day.

That night Susan was reading in the living room when the phone rang. It was Barbara, asking for me.

"I'm afraid Tom isn't back yet from classes," Susan told her. "Can I take a message?"

"Yes, Susan," said Barbara. "Will you tell him that I have been fortunate enough to find an apartment for Mag and me at 25 Brisby Street?"

"Congratulations," Susan said, reaching for a pencil. "Twenty-five Brisby Street," she said, jotting it down. "Do you have a phone?"

"No, I don't, Susan. It hasn't been installed yet."

"Well," said Susan, putting down her pencil. "Tom will be pleased to know you've found a place."

"I'm sure he will be," said Barbara.

There was a pause, and Susan asked how the children's day at school had gone.

"It went fine, thank you."

"Can I speak to them?" Susan asked.

"Speak to them?" Barbara said. "No, I'm afraid you can't speak to them, Susan. They're outside playing."

Susan glanced at the window. It was eight-thirty at night and pitch-dark outside, but Susan wasn't going to press the issue.

"All right then," she said. "I'll tell Tom."

"Thank you, Susan," Barbara said, and hung up the phone.

When I got back that night my response to Barbara's news was relief, and for the first night in a long while I finally got some sleep. I still wished Barbara would move back to Israel, but now at least I could persuade myself that she wasn't planning to snatch the kids. I didn't have any delusions that there wouldn't be any more mischief, but she was putting down roots, building a life for herself, and that was a precondition, it seemed to me, of our coexistence.

Barbara's visitation ended the next morning, and the plan was for the kids to take a taxi to school and ride the bus home in the afternoon.

After I left for my classes that morning a letter came for Ben from his Big Brother back in New Hampshire, and at three o'clock that afternoon Susan strolled to the bus stop to deliver it to him. But when the bus pulled up, and the doors swung open only Geoffrey, their earnest neighborhood pal, stepped off.

As the bus began to pull away Susan knocked on the side and the driver stepped on the brakes.

"Don't do that, lady," he said, swinging the door open again. "Christ. I thought I'd hit somebody."

Susan apologized as the driver, a thin man in a porkpie hat, angrily blew his nose. "Isn't this the bus from Alden Elementary?"

"That's right," he said.

"Aren't Ben and Sara supposed to be on this bus?"

"Ben and Sss—you mean the new kids? The redheads? I call them the redheads."

"Yes. Didn't they get on?"

"No, lady. They didn't get on. I don't know what happened."

"Did they have to stay late for something?"

"I tell you I don't know. Why don't you call the school? I gotta go," and with that he closed the doors and drove off.

Two blond boys waved at Susan through the rear window as she watched the bus turn down Grove Street.

"You want to know about Ben and Sara?"

Susan looked around, and there was Geoffrey in his thick glasses with Scotch-taped frames, staring up at her from the roadside.

"Do you know where they are?" Susan asked.

"Yeah," said Geoffrey. "I know. Their mom came this morning and took them to the . . . pee-dietician."

"Are you sure?"

"I'm sure," said Geoffrey. "Mrs. Lagel lets me help her in the front office. Their mom came in and said they had a appointment."

Susan thanked Geoffrey and ran back to the house to find the phone ringing. It was Mrs. Lagel, the school secretary, calling to say that Barbara had come in early that morning, just after the principal's announcements, claiming that she and Osborne had arranged for her to take Ben and Sara to the pediatrician.

"And you let her take them?" Susan asked.

"Uh, pardon me, Miss Peale," said Mrs. Lagel. "But she *is* the children's mother . . ."

Susan hung up on Mrs. Lagel and tried to calm herself. Maybe Barbara *had* cleared it with me, and I had simply forgotten to tell her about it. Susan picked up the phone again and tried to reach me at the university, but she realized she didn't know which class I was in that evening nor even which department.

She decided to assume that Barbara had told Mrs Lagel the truth: she had taken the children to the pediatrician, but then it had gotten late, and she'd simply kept them with her for the rest of the day. It was a hot afternoon; maybe she'd taken them back to the motel for a swim.

So Susan got into the car and drove to the Dunrollin, wondering how she could avoid a fight with Barbara. Might it be enough just to make sure they were at the motel? Or was she going to have to confront Barbara and fetch Ben and Sara back to the house?

When she reached the Dunrollin the pool had been emptied, and Mr. Garafolo, the proprietor, was cleaning the bottom with a mop.

"Mr. Garafolo," said Susan, "have you seen the kids?"

"No, miss, I haven't. Not since this morning."

"She was with them this morning?"

"Yes, miss. Came by and paid her bill. Said she was moving. But Mrs. Garafolo says she left a pile of stuff. Would you mind taking a look?"

Mr. Garafolo heaved himself up the swimming ladder and showed Susan to Barbara's room. Mrs. Garafolo had obviously tidied things up, but there were clothes, toys, blankets, a lamp, and a stack of book boxes jammed into one corner.

"She can leave the stuff a little while," said Mr. Garafolo. "Not so much demand for rooms this time of year. Or maybe Mr. Osborne could come pick them up if she don't come back?"

"Mr. Garafolo, I'm new to Alden," said Susan, hurrying back to the Volvo. "Where's Brisby Street?"

"Brisby Street, Miss? Hey, it's right there," he said, pointing across the road.

Susan thanked Mr. Garafolo and jumped into the car. Barbara had said that her apartment was number 25 Brisby Street. The street was lined with little green and brown cottages from the 1960s, a few of them winterized by retired working people. Woodpiles, supermarket lawn chairs, and second cars occupied the little yards.

Susan counted the numbers as she drove along: *17, 19, 27, 31* . . . Where was 25?

She pulled into the driveway of number 27, a new house on a wide lot with an overgrown lawn, and peered into the backyard; maybe number 25 was in back.

"Can I help you?" a lady asked from the porch.

"Yes," said Susan. "I'm looking for number 25. A—a friend moved in today with her two children."

"This is 27, dear. There's no 25. Not since the fire took the three houses. That was thirty years ago."

"But she said it was number 25."

"Well," said the woman, stepping indoors, "I'm sure I don't know."

Susan gripped the fence post for a moment. Did she have the number right? Could it have been 35, or 45? She walked down the street and rang the doorbell at number 35, but there was no one home except a small dog yapping from behind the curtained windows. Susan walked around back to look for an apartment, and an elderly man in green pants and a ball cap called out to her from next door.

He said that the house was the Petersons', and he knew for sure that they didn't take boarders, and no, he hadn't seen a woman with three children move in anywhere today, and besides there weren't any apartments he knew of on the whole street.

"Are you sure?" asked Susan, hurrying to her car.

"As sure as I can be," he said with a sniff, "born and raised on Brisby Street."

Late that afternoon Susan finally got through to me at school. At first I couldn't believe it and kept grilling Susan about this or that explanation and saying, "Are you sure? Are you absolutely positive?" to all her answers. "Maybe you got the address wrong."

"I keep wondering that myself, but I *know* she said Brisby Street. Twenty-five Brisby Street."

"Look," I said, digging for my car keys. "I'm on my way. But maybe she did take them to the pediatrician after all. Call him. His name is Dr. Burstyn. He must be in the book."

As I floored it back to Alden I tried to calm myself with the now familiar mantra: *Barbara can't have taken the kids. She could never get away with it. She doesn't have the brains, the will, the guts. She doesn't even want the kids, for Christ's sake. She can't take them to Israel. She can't get passports without my signature. She's just throwing her weight around again. She's just making trouble.*

By the time I'd gotten home, Susan had called Dr. Burstyn, and a

Dr. Morton and a Dr. Simpson and every other pediatrician in the area. None of them had seen the kids.

I began to call all the hotels and motels we could think of, but I came up empty, so we started on the airlines.

We assumed that they could just run a name through a computer, but they couldn't, or in any case wouldn't. It was always, "I'm sorry, sir, but we are not at liberty to give out that information."

"Look," I told TWA. "Somebody has taken my *children*. Why can't you just give me the information?"

But they refused.

By eleven o'clock that night I'd given up on the airlines. I kept thinking of the kids' birthday, kept looking across the kitchen at all the stuff Susan had put together for Ben and Sara's party: candy, favors, noisemakers, and bags of balloons.

I never did get to sleep that night. Every time I heard a car approach I'd bolt to the window. Sometimes, just as I seemed to drift off, I would hallucinate gravel crunching in the driveway or headlights beaming down the wall, and I would lurch out of bed again.

I kept telling Susan that Barbara was just showing off. "She's told herself that she's got a right to her kids, and to hell with the arbitration. She's taken the kids to Marcus for a birthday party in Boston somewhere, just to show me she's still in charge." The next day I would go to the school, and they would be there.

"Just try to get to sleep," Susan told me, beckoning me back into bed, but every time I closed my eyes I saw the widow Folkes again, veering down the street.

By eight o'clock the next morning I was at the door of the Alden school, waiting for Barbara and the kids to show. By eight-thirty the buses had lined up and emptied out along the curb. When the morning bell rang I went to their classrooms to see if they might have gotten by me in the throng, but their chairs were empty.

I marched to the principal's office and was met by the secretary, Mrs. Lagel, a hoarse, chain-smoking woman who greeted me warily as I shoved my way through a congregation of teachers.

"My kids aren't here," I told her. "I checked their rooms. Ben and Sara aren't here. Their mother's taken them."

"Yes, Mr. Osborne," she said. "I called your girlfriend yesterday."

"My girlfriend," I said, glaring at her. "Right. Terrific. You called her about four hours too late. Where the hell is Lepke?"

Mrs. Lagel squinted and pursed her lips at me as everyone else shut up around us, and then Lepke himself appeared in his office door.

"Mr. Osborne," he said. "What can we do for you?"

"My ex-wife's taken my kids. She took them from your school yesterday and she hasn't brought them back."

"Well," said Lepke, ushering me into his office, "I think it may be a little premature to decide she's actually *taken* them," he said comfortably. "Maybe there's merely been a—"

"How could you let this happen? I asked you to keep an eye out for them. And you didn't even check with me about this doctor's appointment story until it was too late."

"Look, Mr. Osborne," said Lepke, losing his patience. "Maybe we've got a communication problem here. But I believe I did tell you that without a court order—"

There was no point in wasting any more time on Lepke, so I turned and drove back to the house. I suddenly knew in my bones that Barbara had abducted the kids; none of the other wishful scenarios made sense anymore.

"They weren't there," I said, hurrying past Susan and rushing for the phone. "I'm calling the police."

Twenty minutes later an Alden police cruiser was pulling into the driveway.

A slight young cop with sunglasses and a peach-fuzz mustache climbed out, all padded up with a down vest and a belt-load of gear: a .38 Smith & Wesson in a creaking leather holster, a billy club, a notepad, and a two-way radio that hissed and squawked as he rang the doorbell. I caught myself thinking how much Ben would have loved to check out the young cop's gear as I welcomed him at the door, but for myself I hated the sight of these artifacts of crime and crisis entering my home.

He introduced himself as Patrolman Andy Flynn, and I showed him to a wing chair, but he couldn't fit himself and his equipment between the arms and had to sit far forward, like an earnest schoolboy at a master's tea, as I tried to fill him in.

"Do you think she's taken them to another state?" he asked, and I mentioned some possible destinations: her mother in Colorado and some friends in New Hampshire and a buddy of hers back in Washington State.

"But you mentioned Israel, Mr. Osborne," Flynn said, hunching over his notebook. "Couldn't she have taken them there?"

"No," I said. "See, I'm their custodial parent. She couldn't have gotten passports for the kids without my signature."

Flynn looked dismayed by this, and thinking he'd somehow missed the point I began to repeat myself.

"No, I get what you're saying, Mr. Osborne," he said gently. "But are you sure about the signature part?"

"What do you mean?" I said uneasily. "I've got legal custody."

Flynn gave me a placating nod. "I'm sure you're right, Mr. Osborne," he said. "What you say makes sense. But where's your phone? Maybe we'd better check this out with the passport office."

So Flynn went to the kitchen and called a Boston passport official and Susan and I looked at each other as he listened to the reply, wearily rubbing his eyes.

"Yeah, I understand," he said. "Mr. Osborne's right here. You can tell him directly."

A man on the other end introduced himself as Mr. Davidson. "Uh, Mr. Osborne, in answer to Officer Flynn's inquiry, we see from our records that passports were indeed issued to Benjamin and Sara Osborne."

"But how can that be?" I said. "I'm their custodial parent. I didn't give my signature."

Davidson hemmed and hawed and said that, well, America didn't really have any provision covering this kind of situation. It was a new problem, and as things stood either parent could request a passport under special circumstances.

"If you want to prohibit us from issuing passports for the kids," he said, "you would have to file a request with the passport agency, but even then it wouldn't be binding without a court order."

It was too late for that, of course. "When did she do it?" I asked. "When did she get the passports?"

I could hear Davidson tapping on a terminal on the other end.

"August," he said finally. "August 9th. I'm terribly sorry, Mr. Osborne. But if it's any comfort I want you to know that your problem is not unique."

So Barbara had been planning to snatch them ever since she got back, and if it hadn't been for the check she'd left behind, she would have snatched them that Sunday before the arbitration.

"Oh Jesus," I said. "What do we do now?"

"What about the FBI?" Susan asked.

I glanced over at Flynn. "That might be helpful," he said with a shrug.

So I dialed information and called the number for the FBI in Boston. The agent who answered heard me out in silence, and when I was finished he cleared his throat and asked if the kids were in danger.

"I don't know," I said. "They're with their mother. But if she's taken them to Israel . . ."

"What I need to know, Mr. Osborne," he said, "isn't whether they're not brushing their teeth regularly. I need to know whether their *lives* are in danger."

"But how can I know that if I don't even know where they are?"

"You see, Mr. Osborne," he continued equably, "the federal kidnapping statute requires that you first demonstrate that your children are in mortal danger before you can involve the FBI."

"But how can I demonstrate—"

"And above and beyond that, Mr. Osborne, we can't act on the complaint of a private citizen. We have to work with the U.S. Attorney who will only work with your local district attorney. Do you see what I mean, Mr. Osborne? We want to help, but we have to follow procedure."

"Can you prove they're in danger?" I asked Flynn after I hung up.

"I think so," said Flynn. "Sounds to me like they're in danger from what you tell me about your former wife. But first we've got to know if they're in Israel."

"But that's what we wanted the FBI to help us find out," said Susan.

Flynn shrugged. "If they're in Israel," he said, "I guess I'm going to need to call the airport in—where?"

"Tel Aviv," Susan told him.

"Tel Aviv, right," Flynn said, leaning over the kitchen counter and jotting it down. "That would be an international call. I guess I'd better check with my chief first."

I asked him if he had a passport.

"A passport? Gee, no," he said.

"You'd better have one," I said. "You may have to go over there and get them."

"Yeah, I guess so," said Flynn, jotting some more. "But, uh, where would I go to get one?"

I figured Flynn wasn't going to get me anywhere, and as soon as he was out the door I called Peter Hill.

"So she really took them, huh?" Hill said after a long pause. "Well, what can I do for you, Tom?"

I looked across the room at one of Sara's drawings hanging askew on the refrigerator. "Peter, help me," I said.

For a moment I could hear Hill puffing on his pipe. "You know, Tom," said Hill, "sometimes private investigators can be useful in this sort of thing."

"Anything," I said. "Do you know any?"

"Well, we have done some business with a man named Donegan. Pat Donegan. A former Boston detective, I understand. What do you think?"

"Yes," I said. "Fine. Can you set it up?"

"Set it up?" said Hill, sounding a little startled. I could hear his chair creak as though he were sitting forward. "Why, yes. I suppose I could. Yes, Tom," he said finally. "I'll do it. Leave it to me."

After Hill signed off I called Bowles up in New Hampshire and told him the news.

"If I were you, Tom," he said, "I would get together some friends and cover the airport."

"But I can't get through to the airlines. They won't tell me anything. What about the FBI?"

"Gee, I don't know, Tom," Bowles said. "It seems to me this is a time for a little self-help."

But what did he mean by self-help? Barbara had been gone for hours. What was I supposed to be doing that I wasn't already doing? Where was I supposed to start? Logan airport? The bus terminal? The train station? Or was I supposed to assign my friends to all the bridges and toll plazas of the greater Boston area?

So that was the extent of my legal advice that first day.

But I had to hand it to Hill; within half an hour his man Donegan was on the phone, and I'd begun to lay out the story.

"Mr. Hill told me a lot of that stuff," he broke in. "Look, Tom, I'm going to help you. I don't know what they told you at P. O. and L., but I've handled a lot of these things. Something like this happens, and you think you're the only one. Am I right? Well, forget it. This thing's an epidemic. Mommies stealing kiddies. Daddies stealing kiddies. It happens all the time."

"The first thing I've got to know, Mr. Donegan, is when Barbara and the kids took off."

"Hey, Mr. Osborne. You don't get anywhere in this business without contacts at the airport. I'll make a call."

"What about finding out if they landed in Israel?"

"No problem," said Donegan. "I got contacts in Israel. Guys who can cut through the tape over there. Consider it done."

I mentioned Marcus.

"Mr. Osborne, are you pulling my leg?" said Donegan. "Somebody send you in here just to make me look good? I got contacts there too. Diamond market in New York is a bitch to penetrate, but I know a guy—I know two guys—they're New York cops. Detectives, homicide. Remember when they started bumping off those little diamond merchants? That was their case. They know the district backwards and forwards. If there's a Marcus in the diamond business they'll find him.

"I'm going to need startup money," he said. "Five hundred should do it. Standard procedure. Then we'll see what we will see."

"The important thing is that we don't want Barbara to find out we're on her trail," I said.

"Check," Donegan said.

"I don't want her to think that we know where she is. I don't want her to bolt."

"You got it, Mr. Osborne," said Donegan. "Believe me, she won't suspect a thing. I'll get started on this right away, but I'm going to need documents."

"What kind of documents?"

"Birth certificates, your custodial agreement, school records, pictures of course, a sample of your ex-wife's handwriting—anything I can put to use here."

"Right," I said.

"In the meantime," said Donegan, "I want you to comb your phone bills, credit card slips, whatever, and see if she made any calls, any charges that might lead us somewhere. You got any of that kind of stuff?"

As it turned out, we did. Susan reminded me that I'd thrown a stack of August bills into a box that still lay unopened in the closet.

Sorting through it we found one of Barbara's bills that must have gotten shuffled in with my mail. It was from a Boston storage firm that turned out to be holding some of Barbara's stuff.

The manager was very cooperative and informed me that she'd called a few weeks back to say that she would be asking him to relay her stuff to Israel, but that she'd never given them an address and was beginning to amass a sizable bill.

"You gonna take care of it?" the manager asked. "I mean, she being your wife and everything."

"*Ex,*" I said, and asked if he would let me know immediately if she got in touch with him again.

He sighed and said, "Yeah. No problem."

Poring over the August phone bill we found a Manhattan number.

"It's got to be Marcus," I said to Susan. "Let's try it."

"Empress Gems," an elderly man with a thick Yiddish accent answered.

I stuck up my thumb and nodded to Susan. "Yes," I said, trying to sound authoritative. "May I speak to Marcus?"

"Wait a minute," the old man said, and in the pause that followed I tried to marshal my wits. What was I going to do? Threaten him? Plead with him?

"Hello," a second, younger voice said. "Who is this?"

"Marcus?"

"Marcus? You want to speak to Marcus?" he asked peevishly.

"Marcus who? Who is this? There's no Marcus here. What do you want with this Marcus?"

I couldn't leave my name and number, nor begin to explain my business, and in my confusion I slammed down the receiver.

"You're over your heads," Uncle Henry told me when I hurried to his house, where he was recuperating from a burst vessel in his right eye. "You're going to get the kids back, but damn it you've got to get a leg up on the process. You've got to speed up getting a warrant out on her or it's just going to drag through the system and get you nowhere.

"But remember, Tom," he said with his hand on my shoulder, "you're going to get them back. You're going to get them back from Barbara, and when you do she's never going to screw you up again."

I hurried back to the cottage to see if Susan had heard anything and found a couple of strange cars parked in the driveway. My heart leaped up—Barbara had brought them back.

I ran into the house and burst into the living room, shouting the children's names, only to find several mothers sitting with their children in their party clothes.

"Oh no," I said. "The birthday party."

"Tom," one of the mothers said, ushering her daughter toward the door. "We're so sorry."

Susan pulled me out into the backyard and handed me a little purple envelope.

"This just came," she said. "I haven't opened it."

The envelope was addressed to me in Barbara's handwriting and postmarked Boston.

"Oh God," I said, ripping it open and reading the following note:

Thomas,
By the time you get this letter you will know that I have left and taken the children with me.
It seems there's to be no truce between us. You have left me no choice.
I will be in touch with you when I can and where I can so

you will know how everyone is. Probably not regularly, but often enough. I expect we will be traveling every so often.

In my wallet I have your address & telephone number (as well as my mother's). If anything should happen to me, you'll be notified immediately.

                                                                    Barbara

Susan and I staggered around a while, trying to make sense of it, searching for clues, for loopholes, for contradictions. It was written on pale pink stationery with a unicorn rearing in the corner. *No truce. No choice. We will be traveling.*

"Can we light the rockets now, Mr. Osborne?"

I turned around, and there was Geoffrey, who had come without his parents.

"You said we were going to light the rockets," he said, sliding his defective spectacles up his nose.

"All right, Geoffrey," I said finally, and led him to the boathouse to fetch the rockets.

A vestigial congregation of mothers and children had gathered on the sloping lawn. They took shy sips of beer and sodas now as Geoffrey and I propped the rockets in little lengths of pipe and bleakly lit the fuses.

The two rockets trembled and sputtered up into the gray afternoon, and as their parachutes opened over the water, a vagrant wind carried them off across the bay.

10

HABEAS CORPUS

I suppose it follows that if you can't remember pain you can't anticipate it, either. Back during the divorce I had sometimes tried to imagine what it would be like if Barbara took Ben and Sara from me, but even at my most morbid I hadn't come close.

When the bond with your children is severed you can succumb to the pain or deny it, or try to put it to work, but it's always there, seeping into everything like a fog. I came from a long line of deniers, but that evening as Susan wrapped the children's birthday cakes and set them in the freezer I decided that if I was ever to see my children again I was going to have to put my pain to work.

I knew that if I tried to take in the full dimension of what Barbara had done it would eat me alive. So I tried to approach my search as a series of containable problems whose solutions, link by link, would lead me to my children.

Sitting up in bed that night I began to check through my address book, trying to think of friends and contacts who could help me find Ben and Sara, and the first to come to mind were the Boczeks.

An old friend of mine from my Providence period, Sam Boczek had recently been elected to the legislature. Sam was a wonderful cigar-chewing politico who, if he weren't so scrupulous, could have stepped straight out of Damon Runyon. His wife Megan was a constituent services staffer for the local congressman, and between them they knew just about everyone in politics. So early the next morning

I rang their doorbell, and they greeted me in their bathrobes and listened to my story at the breakfast table.

Megan took a lot of notes and told me she would call and try to get the state police on the case. And Sam switched immediately into high gear. He told me that if Barbara had taken the children overseas I was going to need the services of the State Department and the FBI, and the only way I was going to get them involved was to get a Massachusetts warrant out for her arrest on a charge of kidnapping a related minor child.

The procedure for obtaining a warrant was simple enough. Flynn had already sworn out a complaint the day before, and now it was a matter of the clerk signing it and sending it along to the local D.A.

The trouble was that the parental abduction statute was brand new, and there was a danger that the court and the D.A. might tell us to come back in two weeks, when we'd be sure Barbara wasn't going to bring the kids back. Or worse—they could treat it merely as a custody dispute, a family matter with which they didn't want to get involved.

Sam called up the Lyman county court in Hammond and asked the clerk, an old army buddy, to draft a warrant right away for Flynn to take to Rick Yantorno, the local assistant D.A. As Susan and I drove to Yantorno's office I felt as though I was really getting somewhere. Others might have trouble animating the system, but I had friends in high places, and for the first time it occurred to me that all of my friends and connections might amount to a kind of pull. Or maybe it would be more accurate to say that for the first time I realized that I had always assumed that, for better or for worse, the system was designed to help and protect the likes of me.

There were five district courts in Lyman county. Defendants indicted by grand juries appeared before the superior court in the city of Lyman, the county seat, while each of the district courts handled minor felonies and misdemeanors.

Assistant D.A. Yantorno's bailiwick was the Hammond district court, where he handled a caseload consisting primarily of the breaking-and-entering cases that predominated in the summer colonies, plus the usual miscellany of drug deals, assaults, and traffic violations. A short, perky man with blow-dried hair and a choirboy's smile, he kept Susan and me waiting only briefly and greeted us graciously enough.

He had obviously spoken both to Flynn and to Boczek, but at first he seemed reluctant to get involved, and gave me the third degree about Barbara.

Okay, he said, so she'd taken the kids; she was their mother, after all. Who said she's unfit? How had she been unreliable? How could I be so sure she wasn't going to bring the kids back tomorrow?

I sort of sputtered away about her threats, about her getaway to Israel and selling the coins and getting the passports and the phony address and all the rest of it. Yantorno listened noncommittally, taking only a few notes as I tried to demonstrate my fitness and the dangers the children faced in Barbara's care.

I handed him copies of the custody agreement and notes from Hill and Bowles about the coins, but it wasn't until Yantorno laid eyes on Barbara's letter that he seemed to sit up and take notice.

"Wait a minute," he said, shaking his head. "What does she mean, 'traveling every so often'? How are the kids supposed to go to school if she's hauling them all over the place?"

"Exactly," I said. "And look—"

"And what's this about probably not communicating regularly? That worries me, Mr. Osborne. That doesn't sound very satisfactory to me.

"This is very good," he said, holding up the letter. "This is evidence. This is something I can take to a judge."

Yantorno went into a long exposition about the special feeling he said he had for cases in which children were the victims. Even as a teenager he'd had a way with children: coaching teams and managing play yards and counseling at summer camps. His office had been handling a spate of child molestation cases that had been flushed out by a new victim/witness program and recent legislation that required social workers to report cases of child abuse to his office. So he saw himself as an advocate of children's rights in the legal system, he said, and these cases broke his heart. One of his great frustrations as a prosecutor was the court's clumsy and insensitive approach to children.

"Look," he said, leaning toward me. "I hope I haven't been giving you a hard time, Tom. Can I call you Tom? But I'm the kind of person who likes to have all the facts lined up so that when I make a decision I know not only what I'm doing but what to expect. What you're asking me to sign is very serious business, Tom. We're talking about a felony warrant. We're talking about possible extradition from a foreign country. We're talking about a fine, maybe even jail for your ex-wife if we find her. So I've got to have my ducks in a row.

"We've got a new statute in Massachusetts that covers this kind of thing," he said, swiveling around and picking up a statute book from the shelf behind him. "It used to be that we had to go after these types of situations under the general kidnapping statute, only that statute included all kinds of language about the victims being held against their wills, when very often the kids felt okay about being with their mom or their dad or whoever.

"But now we've got this new statute," Yantorno said, leafing through the statute book and pausing. "Yeah," he said finally, laying the book down on the desk in front of him. "Here it is. This is Section 26A of Chapter 265 of the General Laws, as amended just this year," Yantorno said, and he began to read.

"Whoever, being a relative of a child less than eighteen years old, without lawful authority, holds or intends to hold such a child permanently or for a protracted period, or takes or entices such a child from his lawful custodian, or takes or entices from lawful custody any incompetent person or other person entrusted by authority of law to the custody of another person or institution shall be punished by imprisonment in the house of correction for not more than one year or by a fine of up to one thousand dollars, or both.

"Now here's the part we're talking about," he said, glancing at me.

"Whoever commits any offense described in this section by taking or holding said child outside the commonwealth or under circumstances which *expose the person taken or enticed from lawful custody to a risk which endangers his safety* shall be punished by a fine of not more than five thousand dollars, or by imprisonment in the state prison for not more than five years, or by both such fine and imprisonment.

"So," said Yantorno, slamming the book shut, "you see why I've got to be convinced the kids are in danger? If they're in danger that ups the ante, that takes it from a one-year maximum misdemeanor to a five-year felony. That puts some teeth in this warrant you're after."

"Well," Susan said, "if you need more documentation . . ."

"I will when I go to the Feds with this thing," he said, holding up his hand. "But not now. After you work at my job for a while, dealing with people and listening to their problems, you develop a pretty good sense right at the beginning whether they're handing you a line of crap or if the matter is serious enough, and they're credible individuals. And Tom, you come across as a very credible individual."

"Thanks, Mr. Yantorno," I said.

"Rick," he said.

"Rick," I said.

"You're a concerned parent, and you're concerned for the safety of your children, and I don't like the sound of this Barbara at all. I don't like what she did with the coins. I don't like this guy Marcus she's taken up with.

"So," said Yantorno, withdrawing a pen from his jacket, "I'm going to sign off on a warrant for Barbara's arrest on charges of kidnapping a related minor. We're going to prosecute Barbara, Tom, and we're going to get back those kids."

"Rick," I said, "it's really just the kids I want. I don't need to prosecute Barbara. All I want is Ben and Sara."

"I understand, Tom, but you've got to look at this from a legal standpoint now," he said. "This isn't just a glorified custody case. We're talking about a crime. Whether it's kidnapping a minor child or a minor relative, it's a heinous crime.

"Somebody's got to think about the kids' rights in this thing," he said, tapping his pen on his desk. "The kids' rights have been violated. These kids have been abducted against their interest and against their will. They're victims of a crime, and if I'm going to pursue this case the perpetrator is going to be prosecuted."

I swallowed hard and looked over at Susan.

"It's the only way to proceed, Tom," Yantorno said with a shrug. "If she's taken the kids overseas we're going to need the Feds to help us bring her back. And you know yourself they aren't going to do anything without a warrant from me."

There was no question that a part of me wanted to see Barbara prosecuted and punished, but I had already determined that if I gave my anger full rein it could foul up my effort to find the kids. Putting my pain to work meant denying how angry I was at Barbara. Because at some crucial stage, the purposes of finding the children and getting back at Barbara would come into conflict. What I wanted first and foremost was the children, and it didn't matter to me if it meant letting Barbara off the hook.

But if Yantorno was my only hope of getting the federal government to make a simple phone call, and if the prospect of prosecuting Barbara was what it was going to take to animate Yantorno, I figured I had no choice but to cooperate.

"All right, Rick," I told him as we shook hands.

"Don't worry, Tom," he said, rising to his feet. "I'm going to send this stuff off to the FBI tomorrow. We'll get your children back."

I called Hill to tell him about my success with Yantorno, but he seemed uninterested.

"I'm not sure you're in the right court there, Tom," he suggested gently. "It seems to me your best bet is to get in touch with a lawyer over in Israel, and maybe a private investigator, and pursue this thing as a civil matter."

"But it isn't a civil matter, Peter," I told him. "She's kidnapped my kids. What's a civil proceeding going to get me? If she's taken them overseas I'm going to need the state behind me. I'm going to need the State Department and the FBI and the U.S. Attorney."

"I suppose," Hill said reluctantly. "But I wouldn't put too much faith in—"

"Look," I said, cutting him off, "if they don't come through for me I'll do whatever I have to do. But if that means going over there and picking up the kids, then I'm going to need information. I'm going to need someone to take the lead in this thing. I need to know what the legal situation is going to be over there."

"Well, my guess is—"

"Do you know of any Israeli lawyers, Peter?"

"Not offhand," said Hill.

"How about your New York office? Wouldn't they know of any?"

"They might. Yes," said Hill. "They just might. I'll give them a call and see what they can tell me.

"In the meantime I've been thinking this over, Tom," Hill continued. "We're going to need writs of *habeas corpus* on Barbara and the kids."

"How do we get those?"

"Well, first I better file a petition to enforce a foreign judgment."

"What's that?"

"That means we take the Vermont custody ruling, and we get it enforced in Massachusetts probate court."

"And then?"

"Well," he said, "once we've changed the venue of the custody ruling we can file a petition of complaint because she's taken them out of the commonwealth, and the court will issue writs of *habeas corpus* ordering her to appear."

"But I've already got a felony warrant issued on her."

"Well, Tom," said Hill, "you can go your own way on this if you like, but this is what I as your lawyer would advise doing. The court will order her to appear, and if she doesn't appear she'll be in violation."

"She's already in violation," I began to say, but I choked myself off. Maybe Hill was right. Maybe we were both right. Maybe the thing to do was to attack this problem from all sides at once.

Flynn came by around three o'clock to report that he had gotten his chief's permission to call Tel Aviv airport, but that as a small-town cop he couldn't cut it with the airport police.

Flynn had managed, however, to persuade El Al and TWA to review their passenger lists, and they had no record of Barbara and the kids on any of their flights, and none of the local travel agencies had heard of her either.

Mrs. Garafolo at the Dunrollin told Flynn that during the weekend Barbara had reported that she had found a house to rent in town and that she and the kids would be moving out of their room on

Tuesday the 13th. But early Tuesday morning Barbara had stopped by the office to report that it was going to take her a little longer than she'd expected to move, so she wanted to pay in advance for one more night's lodging at the Dunrollin.

She and the kids had then taken off in a cab, and Mrs. Garafolo didn't see any of them again until two o'clock that afternoon when Mag showed up alone in another cab and collected half a dozen suitcases from their room. The last thing Mrs. Garafolo remembered was a glimpse of Mag riding off in the taxi; she seemed to be crying.

"Oh God," I said. "Poor Mag. Well, what about the cab company? Where did they take her?"

Flynn said he had found a driver at the local cab company who remembered taking Barbara and the kids to a restaurant called Gildy's on the Monday before they disappeared. The cabby even recalled her mentioning that she'd found a house to rent on Brisby Street and that she had just received some money she'd been waiting for. But there was no record of her having taken one of their cabs on the day of the kidnapping.

It seemed to me that contriving to use a cab from another town was too clever for Barbara; she'd covered her tracks too well to have acted alone. I became convinced that Marcus was behind these elaborate ploys and deceptions.

But if so, Marcus must have run things from a distance. Flynn said that no one—not Mrs. Garafolo, not the cabby, not the waitress at Gildy's—ever saw Barbara with a male companion.

While Flynn was at the house Megan Boczek called to say that she'd spoken to an official named Barker in the Massachusetts Office of Public Safety who informed her of a new state police missing-persons unit. Barker had told Megan that he would call Mary Ramirez, the trooper in charge, and tell her to expect a call from Flynn and me. So after I thanked Megan I gave Ramirez's name and number to Flynn.

"Missing-person's unit?" he said. "I really don't think the state police do much investigating of missing persons."

But I wasn't going to put up with any intergovernmental rivalry at my expense. "Look, Andy," I said, "you don't understand. This is a new unit. We're dealing with the top levels of the department here. The commissioner himself is on the case. I want us to work with them."

"Okay," he said, dubiously writing down the number. "I suppose it can't hurt."

Late that afternoon Donegan reported that he had made an appointment to meet with his contacts at Logan airport and would be checking back with me just as soon as he learned something. He also suggested that Susan call Visa posing as Barbara and ask that in the future all of her bills be sent to our address in Alden. That way if she made any charges on her card we could trace her movements.

We figured that with Barbara's tendency to be careless with money she would eventually have to employ her charge card, so we thought this was a terrific idea. Visa fell for Susan's act and promised to send future bills to us.

Hill called to say that he'd found an Israeli lawyer named Saul Geva who had evidently handled cases like mine in the past.

"Just to review," Hill said, "what exactly is it we need from him?"

"Well," I said, "to begin with, it seems to me we've got to know if Israel's going to recognize me as custodial parent."

"Right," said Hill.

"And I guess I also need to know if she's going to be able to apply for citizenship on their behalf under the Law of Return."

"Law of Return. Right. Okay," he said. "I'll cable him right away."

All of this had been accomplished in a single day, and as Susan and I went to bed I felt as though we'd finally set some wheels in motion. But merely passing by Ben's and Sara's rooms was enough to jolt me out of my hubris. Barbara had taken away my children, and now they were in danger. If only I'd been more vigilant they might still be safe at home.

11

ON THE CASE

I was ready to spend every penny I had to retrieve my children. I was prepared to throw over everything: quit school, pack my suitcase, and wander the world, if that's what it was going to take.

But first I had to know where the kids were, and where they were depended on whether Barbara was in earnest or merely playing games. It seemed to me that if she were in earnest she could have taken the children anywhere, from Thailand to Finland, from Uruguay to Pakistan. But if she was playing games they were probably in Israel somewhere. All I needed from the FBI was a single phone call to establish whether they'd entered Israel; I was prepared to do the rest.

Susan could see that in order to think clearly I was going to need a home base. She convinced me not to give up school right away; I was going to need the concentrated diversion to keep my head on straight. If it turned out in the end that I couldn't juggle everything at once—couldn't both find my children and go to school—then obviously school was going to have to go. But one way or another we had to maintain at least a modicum of normality. When we got the kids back (and it was always "when" with Susan, never "if"), they needed to return to a home that wasn't utterly centered on their absence. There had to be a life there, and a routine, or we would all go crazy.

On Friday morning Susan found a June bill from a collect call Barbara had made from Israel.

We debated for a good hour whether to give it a try. Susan figured we had nothing to lose, but I was concerned that if we did get through to her she would run with the kids again, and this time she might take them anywhere.

We decided to compromise. Susan would call, but she would disguise her voice and pose as someone from Visa checking on her bill.

So as I listened on the kitchen extension, Susan called the mystery number. It rang shakily for a while, and then a woman answered.

"Hello?" said Susan in a brisk little voice I'd never heard from her before. "This is Visa calling. May I speak to Barbara Kaye Osborne, please?"

There was quite a long pause, and I was afraid we'd been disconnected. But then the woman said something interrogative that sounded like, "You Barbara?"

"Uh, no," said Susan, faltering a little. "This is Visa calling. I want to speak to Barbara Kaye Osborne."

"Joost minute," the woman said, and put down the phone.

I balked at that point, and we slammed down our phones together and gaped at each other for a moment, trying to figure out what had happened.

I was convinced we'd hit the bull's-eye, that the woman had gone to fetch Barbara. But Susan wasn't so sure. Maybe the woman just hadn't understood English and had gone off to fetch someone who did.

Either way, these were slim pickings compared to what we'd managed to accomplish the day before. Everyone was out pursuing this and that, but no one had anything to report, and now the weekend loomed ahead of us.

I came to dread the empty spaces in the week. I could keep my head above water so long as I kept busy, but if the phone didn't ring, if we weren't hot on the trail of some clue, the enormity of my children's absence overcame my resolution, and I would begin to sink.

So Saturday was murder. People couldn't be reached at their offices, no one called in, and all I could do was work through my Rolodex, panning for ideas from my friends.

The one real piece of advice we garnered was from one of Susan's cousins whose child had been abducted by her father. She said that she'd gotten some help from an organization called Child Find that specialized in locating abducted children, and so Susan took down the address and sent away for an application form.

Sunday was even worse than Saturday. The headlines in the *Globe* concerned the marines under siege in Lebanon and the navy shelling the Syrians. I kept thinking about the recent attacks on Israeli settlements and imagining my children somewhere in that grim vicinity, riding the school bus past checkpoints and gun emplacements.

First thing Monday morning I called Donegan to hear what he'd found out at the airport.

"Oh yeah, Mr. Osborne. I was just going to call you. I went out there Friday to see my contact."

"And?"

"Well, I can't say I got that much to tell you, Mr. Osborne."

"Did you find out when they took off?"

"Not really," he said. "You see, this guy I know, this state trooper, he and I sort of missed each other. I got out there, and they couldn't scare him up for me."

"Then what about Marcus? Have you found out anything more about him?"

"Don't worry," said Donegan. "I've got my lines out. I'm on the case."

Flynn still wasn't having any luck getting through to Tel Aviv, so he suggested that I call the Israeli consulate in Boston to see if they might be able to develop some information for us about Barbara's whereabouts in Israel.

Susan and I set off to see the consul himself that afternoon. He was a courtly and enigmatic man named Tisher who heard us out impassively and told us that, yes, he might be able to develop some information about Barbara's arrival, but it was going to have to go through channels. "And channels, as you know, Mr. Osborne, take time."

"How much time?"

"That I can't say," said Tisher. "I'm going to need approval from our various offices."

He shrugged a little when I emphasized how urgently we needed the information, and I could see that there was going to be no spurring him any faster.

We asked whether the Law of Return could possibly be applied to Barbara and the kids and Tisher told us he couldn't advise us about that, but we might check with the Jewish Agency, the main Israeli settlement organization in Boston.

Tisher's assistant, Jean Stein, was more sympathetic and offered to let us pore over the consulate's collection of Israeli phone books to see if we could find any of the Israeli numbers we'd culled from our phone bills and match them with names. But Jean returned from the consulate library with an embarrassed look. She should have remembered, she said: the consulate's phone books were in Hebrew.

When I called the Jewish Agency from home that afternoon I was shunted over to a flack named Shepel who gave me one of the quickest brushoffs I'd ever experienced. A couple of sentences into my little exposition on my children's abduction he broke in to say that he didn't get involved in domestic disputes and wouldn't have any idea how to find the information I was after.

"But it's exactly the kind of information you must have," I said. "You guys have got to know about the Law of Return."

"I can't help you," he said. "I'm sorry. Good-bye." And he hung up the phone.

In the meantime Flynn had gone to the hotel in Boston where Barbara had stayed and persuaded the manager to give him a record of her phone calls.

"There's lots of calls on this bill to Colorado," Flynn told me over the phone. "Who does she know out there?"

"Oh, no," I said. "It's her mother."

There'd been no love lost between Kitty and me, but in recent years she and Barbara hadn't been close either, so it was hard for me to believe that Kitty would have allowed Barbara to draw her into a conspiracy. Nevertheless these calls Flynn had uncovered must have been made just after Barbara's first attempt to take the kids. What else could they have talked about?

So when I called Kitty Wednesday evening I tried to shake her down. I told her that there was a warrant out for Barbara's arrest on the felony charge of kidnapping a related minor child and that anyone who conspired with Barbara was open to all kinds of charges of complicity and obstruction of justice.

But she was all grandmotherly shock and wounded innocence: "Oh goodness, Tom. Oh my dear, I had no idea."

For the time being I decided to play along with it and asked her to review her letters from Barbara to see if she'd mentioned Marcus's last name in any of them. Kitty assured me she would.

On Thursday morning the phone rang, and it was Donegan.

"What have you got?" I said. "Did you find out about Marcus?"

"I'm still working on that, Mr. Osborne. Don't sweat it."

"How about when they took off? Did you talk to the airport?"

"Well, I keep missing my contact at the airport, Mr. Osborne. All I get is an answering machine."

"Then how about when they landed? Have you had any luck with the Israelis?"

"That's really what I'm calling about, Mr. Osborne. I keep calling Israel, and I can't understand anybody. I try to get through to these guys, and nobody knows what I'm talking about."

"Well, can't you get somebody to help? Somebody to translate?"

"Translate what? These are Jews, Mr. Osborne. They speak English."

"Hebrew," I told him. "They speak Hebrew over there."

"*Hebrew,*" said Donegan. "Jesus Christ, Mr. Osborne. I thought it was just a bad connection."

Megan had evidently lit some kind of fire under Barker, the official in the Office of Public Safety, because he called that Friday to say that he'd been in touch not only with Yantorno and the state police, but with Donegan and an agent named Jenkins at the FBI.

Jenkins had told him that in order for the FBI to get involved there had to be some evidence of potential danger or harm to the children.

"What kind of evidence?"

"Well," said Barker, "he didn't go into that. But Rick Yantorno says he's prepared to demonstrate endangerment. In the meantime I've told Trooper Ramirez to get her unit onto this case and contact your Officer Flynn and your man Donegan so they can coordinate this thing."

Donegan called back to report that he hadn't been able to find anyone to translate for him.

"What do you mean?" I asked him. "Your brochure says you've got personnel who speak all kinds of languages."

"Well, Tom, we don't get much call for Hebrew."

"All right," I said. "I'll see what I can do."

So I called Alan Feldman, a Jewish colleague of mine in Bourne who'd watched Barbara's conversion with amused interest.

Alan told me he would call a nephew of his who was a rabbinical student in Brookline and have him contact Donegan directly.

"Barbara's certainly full of surprises, isn't she?" Alan said. "I told you she was *meshugah*."

Donegan called again on Friday.

"Hey, I got through to my guys in New York on this Marcus character."

"And?"

"Well, look, Mr. Osborne. The one thing you got to understand is it's a very closed community down there. It's like the Mafia, you know, a goddamned Jewish Cosa Nostra. Everybody's related, everybody's covering for everybody else, nobody's talking."

"I know," I said. "You told me that already. But what about your cops? What did they tell you?"

"That's who I'm quoting here, Mr. Osborne. That's where I'm getting this stuff. They know the business backward and forward. They say if we got somebody named Marcus in the diamond business we got a serious problem, Mr. Osborne. No question about it."

Hill sent me a copy of the letter he'd sent by courier to Geva. It laid out the circumstances of the children's abduction pretty well, but it seemed to me vague on what specific questions we needed answered, so on Monday, October 3rd I decided to call Geva directly.

Geva himself picked up the phone, and he was very reassuring;

he'd received Hill's initial cable and had already begun to look into the matter.

I told him that I knew that Barbara had applied for citizenship, but I figured that the Law of Return was probably a little dicey for her since she was an unemployed, converted American WASP. Just the same, if Israel had the poor judgment to grant her citizenship, I needed to know whether citizenship would automatically be extended to the children.

"Yes, Mr. Osborne," said Geva. "That's the question. But I know all about this sort of thing. Handle it all the time. We've got to act quickly before she files for custody. If she files for jurisdiction of the children here we'll have to go to court, and it'll just be a big mess."

"But what's the answer to the question?" I asked Geva. "Will they extend citizenship automatically?"

"We have to be very careful, Mr. Osborne," he said. "This can be a very delicate business. What I'm going to do is dig up some cases that apply to your situation, and then we will confer further.

"But don't worry, Mr. Osborne. If they are in Israel we will find them for you."

By now it was easier to think of them in Israel. I couldn't deal with the possibility that they might have gone to Indonesia or Paraguay or some backwater town in Louisiana. It was easier even than imagining them in Canada, where it would be harder to spot two fair red-headed children.

Israel may have been under perpetual siege, but it cared about children, and it had a comprehensive welfare system and a judicial system with continuity and integrity. If we did have to go through the courts we were better off in Israel than, say, El Salvador.

Still, Barbara could just as easily have taken up with a Burmese gem merchant as an Israeli one, and as yet I had no direct evidence that she'd actually taken the children to Israel, only an assumption predicated on her conversion. In fact Israel should have been the last place she would have gone if she were really serious about my not finding Ben and Sara.

I could only hope that for all the trouble and all the risks she'd gone through to demonstrate the ferocity of her motherhood, in the end she would want me to find her and take them off her hands.

12

NOT SO FAST

Susan began to send away to every organization she could find that addressed the problem of missing children, and in time the mail was filled with flyers, application forms, solicitations, handbooks, and directories.

Their logos depicted shadowy men leading weeping children away, teenagers being accosted in bus stations, justice crying, children slipping out of their parents' hands, abandoned teddy bears and sneakers, overturned wagons, balls bouncing into empty streets.

Some of the groups' names conveyed an anguished, entrepreneurial peppiness: For Kids' Sake; H.E.A.R.T. (Help Every Abduction Return Today); Operation Go-Home; and the Hide and Seek Foundation. There were the groups named after other missing children: the Adam Walsh Resource Center; the Committee to Find Etan Patz; the Dee Scofield Awareness Program; the Roberta Joe Society; Edwin Shaw IV, Inc.

There was not only Child Find but Friends of Child Find; Child Search; Child Stealing Resource Center; the Bay Area Center for Victims of Child Stealing; Ident-I-Child; Save-a-Child. There was the Abducted Children Information Center; the Another Mother for Children Foundation; Children's Rights; Family and Friends of Missing Children; Missing Children Help Center; National Missing Children's Locate Center; Sacramento Stolen Children Action Network; Stolen Children Information Exchange; and Top Priority: Children.

The names of the parent groups seemed to sort themselves into a horrifying declension: Parents Against Child Stealing; United Parents Against Child Stealing; Parents Against Child Snatching; Parents Against Legal Kidnapping; Parents Helping Parents; the Searching Parents Organization; Parents of Murdered Children; Parents Alone.

They were full of advice and information, but a lot of it was political and prophylactic: how to lobby for enlightened custody laws, how to prevent abductions. They asked for donations, registration fees, dues, subscriptions. They advertised vanity press publications, fingerprinting kits, mystics and coloring books.

I tried to be heartened by the sheer number of groups working on the problem, but in the aggregate all these organizations improvising out of attics and kitchens and office parks in every state in the union seemed to suggest that mine was an insignificant instance of a national problem of grotesque and insurmountable dimensions.

If there were scores of groups organized around this problem how many other parents were in my shoes? One group asserted that 25,000 children were abducted every year, another put the figure at 750,000 and estimated that 80 percent had been kidnapped by their noncustodial parent. How many custodial parents ever recovered their children? How many had finally given up hope?

"Until we get the state and federal government to stand up and take notice," declared one pamphlet, "there can be no hope for the thousands upon thousands of children abducted every year."

"I'm working on it," I muttered bleakly as I filled out registration forms with descriptions of Ben and Sara, reduced for these purposes to eyes and hair, heights and weights, birth dates, and distinguishing scars.

As I entered the third week without the kids I began to pester the Israeli consulate to see if they'd found out yet whether Barbara had landed in Israel. Jean Stein, the consul's secretary, was always polite and sympathetic but firm. The request had to go through the consul in Boston to the embassy in Washington and then over to Israel's foreign ministry and then back to the police and over to the airport and back up the line to Boston.

"But why can't you just give them a call?" I kept asking.

"No, no," she'd tell me. "It has to go through channels."

While I attended my classes, Susan would go to the library and pore over phone books, trying to match the numbers we had with Marcus or Barbara herself, trying to find his last name, the address for the number we called, anything that might tell us where she was. But none of the numbers matched.

On October 5th I called Rabbi Shapiro back in Bourne on the chance that Barbara might have been in contact with him. He told me he had indeed corresponded with Barbara over the past year but wasn't sure he'd kept any of her letters. I asked him to review his files for me and send me anything that might help me find the kids, but he kept getting more and more vague about his communications with her.

"I just don't know if I have anything for you, Tom," he said.

"Well, could you just check for me? All I'm trying to find is her address."

"Your divorce was such a sad business, Tom," he said uncertainly. "It's such a shame it's worked out this way."

I wasn't yet prepared to confront Rabbi Shapiro, but I was convinced he knew something. If he didn't come through with any information I would have to try to shake him down.

The phone in the kitchen became the nucleus of scrawlings and clutter as we made our desperate calls. The counter was littered with note pads and pamphlets and hundreds of scraps of paper with phone numbers and addresses jotted on them. Making the telephonic rounds of private detective, D.A., consul, lawyer, local cops, state troopers, officials, clerks, psychologists, and secretaries, I developed a kind of numbness in the outer ear and a chronic pain in the neck and shoulder that somebody once diagnosed as receptionist's palsy.

Donegan called to say that he'd gotten hold of Alan Feldman's nephew and that together they'd gotten through to Israel.

"He's a smart kid," said Donegan. "Knows Hebrew. So I put him on the extension. This was yesterday afternoon. So we called. Phone rings—I'm not kidding—maybe a dozen times. Then this guy comes on, and he's real pissed off. Says it's four in the morning.

" 'Hey, sorry,' we say, and he hangs up.

"So this afternoon the kid comes in again, we dial again, and it's the same goddamn thing. Guy says it's four in the morning and hangs up.

"Can you figure that, Mr. Osborne? Four in the morning two goddamn days in a row?"

On October 12 I received a letter from attorney Geva.

Dear Mr. Osborne:
 First of all I will like to give a picture about the legal situation as follows:

1) As an introduction please see the article of the Israeli Law Review hereby enclosed.

2) It's very important to have an habeas corpus from the american court so to enable me to present the american order.

3) I enclose to an Israeli judgment given in similar circunstances which was enforced by an american court.

 Please find enclosed my bill for services so far—$3500.

Yours Sincerely,

Saul Geva
Magister Juris
Advocate–Notary
Tel Aviv*

I read the cases several times, but they didn't answer my question. One case involved a custodial father who'd taken his children to Israel. The Israelis had evidently ruled in the mother's favor, thereby honoring an American ruling that had found the father in contempt of court. The other concerned an Israeli court's decision to allow an Israeli father to retain custody after the mother ran off to the States with her lover.

So the next day I called Hill.

"Yes, I read them too," he said. "Interesting cases."

"But what have they got to do with my case?"

"Oh, I think they're comparable. One of them's from the Israeli Law Review. It's some kind of precedent."

"But it doesn't answer the question, does it?"

"What question is that, Tom?"

"Whether or not they'll honor my custody agreement."

"Well, it indicates that they'll decide on the basis of the good of the children."

"But what does that mean? It doesn't answer the question, Peter."

"Well, no, Tom," said Hill. "I guess if you look at it in that light he's sent the wrong case. But it isn't useless."

"The best you can say is that it isn't useless, and for this he wants thirty-five hundred dollars?"

"I don't know what to tell you, Tom. It seems like a lot of money."

I let Geva's letter drop to the floor. "Then let's dump Geva, Peter. Come on. Let's get something *going* here."

"Wait a second, Tom," said Hill. "Not so fast."

"Look, Peter, what I'm asking is so simple. All I want to know is whether Israel is going to honor my custody agreement. Period. Can't we get an Israeli on the line who can answer that for us?"

"Well, that's what we've been trying to do, Tom," said Hill.

"Then why don't you call your New York office again?"

"I don't know if that'll do much good, Tom. You see, they gave us Geva in the first place."

"But can't they scare up someone else for us? Can't they check somebody out for us this time?"

"Well, all right," said Hill. "I'll send them another memo."

Susan came back from one of her forays into the phone books to report that she'd found the phone number of Mag's boarding school in Hadera. I realized that I'd been concentrating so hard on Ben and Sara that I'd forgotten all about Mag's schooling.

We called and spoke to the headmistress, an Englishwoman named Dunbar. She was very cooperative and shared my concern, because in fact Barbara had enrolled Mag for a second year at her school but Mag had never shown up.

Susan had also found the number of an American school in Hadera, and we called it as well, in case Mag might have transferred. They were less cooperative than Mrs. Dunbar, but they had obviously never heard of Mag or Barbara or the kids.

Visa sent us Barbara's account statement on the 12th of October, but there was no record of her having charged anything. She had paid off her bill of $2800 with her last alimony payment, so the only significance we could draw from the statement was that if you figured in what the trip must have cost, plus how expensive everything was in Israel, plus the Visa bill she'd paid, all compounded by her inexperience with both money and employment, she had to be running low on funds. Unless she was getting help from Marcus, she was eventually going to have to come up for air.

The storage company still hadn't heard from her when we called that same day. "This account is starting to pile up, Mr. Osborne," the manager said. "I'm not going to hold your stuff for you much longer."

"I'm sorry," I told him. "But it's not my stuff and you're not holding it for me."

The next day I called Hill back to see if the New York office had found us a new Israeli.

"Well, Tom," said Hill. "I sent the New York office a memo, but I never got an answer."

So I hung up on Hill and called the Israeli embassy in Washington, where a legal attaché promptly read me a list of five Israeli lawyers who'd represented Americans in Israel.

I drove into Boston and delivered the list to Hill, who met me in his outer office.

"I'm in a meeting, Tom. Can you get back to me on this?"

"I got a list of lawyers for you to call, Peter."

"That's good work, Tom," said Hill. "But I don't think that's exactly a lawyer's business. Why don't you call them?"

"Goddamn it, Peter," I said, stepping toward him. "Because you're the lawyer. I'm paying you to represent me in this. You're supposed to know the issues to talk about."

"All right, Tom, calm down," said Hill, handing the list to his secretary. "I'll call them if that's the way you want to handle it."

In the mail on the morning of October 19th was an itemized bill for $1015 from Donegan for "investigatory services rendered to date."

So I girded my loins and called Donegan. "What investigatory services?" I wanted to know. "You said you were going to talk to some guy at the airport. You couldn't get him. You said you had some contact in Israel. You never got through. You said you had cops who could find out about Marcus. They didn't tell you a thing."

"Hey, Mr. Osborne. Hold on a minute," said Donegan. "I've been acting in good faith here. This is a highly speculative business. You haven't even sent me my retainer. It's not my fault these leads you gave me were dead ends. I can't help that."

"Look," I told him. "I hired you because you said you had all these contacts. You were going to get me through to all these guys and develop some information. You were going to conduct the whole orchestra. And you haven't delivered, Mr. Donegan. Except for the Visa idea you haven't come through with a goddamn thing."

"But I never said I was done. All I'm charging you for is services rendered so far. I'm still on the case."

I sat down on a kitchen stool and hunched over the counter. "No, you're not," I said, closing my eyes.

"Pardon?"

"I said, 'No, you're not.' You're off the case."

"Off the case? What are you talking about?"

"Look, Mr. Donegan," I said, "I know you want to help, but you haven't come up with anything since the credit card idea. You said you had contacts. None of them panned out."

"Yet."

I looked at my calendar. "You've had a month, Mr. Donegan. I've waited four weeks for something from you—*anything*. And you've come up with zero. I've had to find out everything myself and it's cost me time. I'll pay for the first meeting, and I'll pay for your calls to the New York cops, but that's it."

"Look, Mr. Osborne, I don't think you're being exactly fair here."

"No, Mr. Donegan, *you* look," I said, and I realized I'd begun to shake. "My kids are missing. I'm going to need all my resources to find them. You've already wasted my time. You're not going to waste my money."

Susan nodded to me as I hung up the phone. "That was good," she said.

"Yeah," I said. "I'm a real tiger on the phone. But now what the hell do we do?"

I called Hill.

"You fired him?" Peter asked when I broke the news about Donegan.

"That's right, Peter," I said. "The guy was useless."

"So you just let him go?"

"Never mind that, Peter," I said. "Did you call the lawyers on the list?"

"Uh, yes I did, Tom. First thing this morning."

"How many of them did you call?"

"Oh, just the first one, Tom. He seemed fine. He wants some money, but he says he's got what we need to know."

"Well, did you talk to him about the situation?"

"Look," said Hill, "he's not going to talk to me without the money, Tom. You've got to realize how these guys work. He wants thirty-five hundred dollars."

I was beginning to think that $3500 was a magic number, that it was in some Israeli bar association rate book or something. Animating Hill was like pushing a string, and I was beginning to wonder where it was getting me. How was any of this stuff going to help me if I didn't even know where my children were?

So I hung up on Hill and gave up for the time being on the civil track to cast my lot with Yantorno.

13

UFAP

There's a picture I have of Ben and Sara and me that was taken during our last year in Bourne. At the time I was working on a little model boat with Ben when Sara slipped between us to evaluate our progress. So there the three of us are with our fragile little craft. It's a trick of perspective, I suppose, but we all seem to be beaming at each other at once.

I came upon the picture in an album a week after the kids disappeared, and it became a kind of icon. I bought a frame for it and set it up on my chest of drawers next to the boat we'd made, and every time my spirits sagged I would pay a visit to my little shrine.

These pilgrimages didn't cheer me up, exactly, for the best I could manage was a couple of seconds of conjuring them back into my presence before they'd flit off again to parts unknown. But it would always brace me for the next phone call I had to make, the next poor bureaucrat I had to badger.

Shortly after our first meeting Yantorno had abandoned trying to get the FBI to pursue the case on a federal kidnapping warrant.

Evidently the FBI office in Boston had insisted that Yantorno demonstrate that the children's lives were in danger before it could move.

"Tom, I keep asking them how in hell we're supposed to know that unless we find the kids dead on the sidewalk, for crying out loud."

"Jesus, Rick," I said.

"Sorry, Tom. But you see what I mean? What they're supposed to do is get the evidence in front of them, and then they've got to infer. Are they in danger or aren't they? Now, *I* think the kids are in physical danger—maybe not from Barbara directly but from the circumstances she's subjected them to. Right? I mean, she's got no money, she's got no job, she's kooky, and let's face it, Tom; Israel isn't exactly the safest place in the world."

But then a week later he called to say that it turned out that the whole exercise with the federal kidnapping charge had been bullshit to begin with because the statute specifically excluded kidnappings by parents.

"And they never told you that?"

"They told me eventually, Tom," said Yantorno. "But these guys aren't volunteering anything. We've got to get our own ducks in a row on this one."

So Yantorno switched gears. It turned out that there was something called an Unlawful Flight to Avoid Prosecution statute, or UFAP, that evidently required no evidence of endangerment.

"All we've got to demonstrate," Yantorno told me, "is that she fled the state, and then the FBI has got to go after her."

"But what would they go after her for?"

"For fleeing the state. You see, Tom, UFAP's a funny kind of statute because to my knowledge nobody's ever been prosecuted for violating it. It's just this device we've got for getting the Feds on a case.

"Let's say a D.A. thinks a bank robber has left his state. He goes to the U.S. Attorney, and he gets a UFAP warrant. So then the FBI goes after the bank robber and catches him in another state and hands him over to us. Then the Feds just withdraw the UFAP warrant, and we prosecute for bank robbery."

"So if Barbara's a fugitive—"

"Oh, she's a fugitive all right," said Yantorno. "There's a warrant out for her arrest in Massachusetts, and Flynn's put together all this terrific evidence that she's left the state. The clincher for me is her letter. 'I expect we will be traveling' and all the rest of it.

"So there's no doubt about it. We're going after her on a UFAP."

For a while Yantorno was very hopeful. But when nothing seemed to be happening I began to call the FBI myself. I got to know an agent named Jenkins in the Boston office who assured me that just as soon as he got his warrant from the U.S. Attorney he would jump to it.

"I want to help you, Tom," he told me. "But I can't do anything until I've got this warrant from Walsh."*

So naturally I began to call Walsh.

Walsh was a plausible young assistant in the U.S. Attorney's office who in turn assured me that he wanted to help, but he couldn't do anything unless he got a request from Yantorno.

So then I called back Yantorno, and he said, "I don't understand this, Tom. We've been requesting for two weeks now, and every time we send in the application they send it back and tell me it's been improperly filled out."

It turned out that Barker, my contact in the state police, was a former FBI man, so I asked him to help out with the application process. He got right on it, but his forms kept getting sent back too, until he finally went to Walsh's office in person to review the application himself.

When I called agent Jenkins again he said he too was fed up and disgusted with the delays.

"I don't know what's going on with Walsh," he'd tell me. "But I'm going to get after him, Tom. This has gone on long enough.

"But look, Tom," he said. "When I do get my agents on this case I want it clean. I know you're frustrated, but don't go out and do something crazy on your own. I don't want us working at cross purposes.

"I'll tell you what," he said. "Give me the directions to your house, just to save us some time here. I'm going to call Walsh again. I've been bugging them about this, and I'm going to get the darn warrant, and I'm going to send my men down to you and get going on this thing."

So I stood there in my kitchen and gave him the directions: "Take Route 95 to exit so-and-so, turn left onto Route 11 and watch for—" and so on, and I entertained this vision of G-men fanning out across Massachusetts, across America, across the globe, never giving up until they'd found my children.

Now that the application had been properly filled out, Walsh kept telling me that my case was still under review; he was going to have to pass it by his boss, U.S. Attorney Stanley Thorpe. His reassurances that all this was just a formality began to falter, and he began vaguely to suggest that we still needed to demonstrate endangerment.

By this time I was pretty cocky about the legalities. "What are you talking about?" I said. "This is a UFAP warrant we're trying to get. Not a kidnapping warrant. You told us that all we needed to show was that she was out of the state."

"Well, endangerment is part of the picture too."

"Then send me the statute. Show me where it requires endangerment."

"Send you the statute?"

"Yeah. Send me a copy. Show me what it says."

"Tom, I'm afraid I'm just not going to do that. That would be providing legal advice, and I'm afraid that isn't a part of my function."

"So there's nothing in the statute about endangerment, is that it?"

"Well, Tom," said Walsh. "We've got to prioritize, you realize. We've got to be convinced of the urgency of a case before we take it on. I want to help you. That's why we're in this crazy business, right? But there's no use my helping if the FBI isn't going to do anything anyway."

"But Jenkins says he's just waiting for you to okay it."

"I somehow doubt that, Tom. I've talked to Jenkins about this, and he says he's not going to get involved. So what would be the point of my pushing for a warrant?"

I hung up on Walsh and called Jenkins. At first he kept up his portrayal as my frustrated champion, but it got a little thin after a while.

"You know, Mr. Jenkins," I said finally, "when I'm desperate it makes me into a sucker. I begin to believe things because I have to believe them. But you aren't going to do anything for me, are you?"

"Now, Tom."

"You never were going to do anything. And in a way you've been telling me that all this time with this runaround you've been giving me."

"No runaround, Tom," said Jenkins. "You've got to understand. This is a very complicated business."

"But why spin my wheel? Why couldn't you have told me at the beginning that you weren't going to do anything?"

Jenkins sighed and cleared his throat. "All right, Tom, look. We get a lot of these situations. People get very unhappy and frustrated. You're going to get more frustrated. But we all feel good about you, Tom. We all feel you're a nice guy. One of the more pleasant people we've had to deal with. We respect you."

I said, "Well, it's not up to you anyway. It's a legal decision. It's up to Walsh. Let's see what he has to say about this."

And he said, as though I'd missed the point, "All I can say to you, Tom, is that, well, basically we like you."

I was ready to throw in the towel, but Yantorno still held out hope that Walsh would approve the UFAP warrant.

"He's not going to let Jenkins drive this thing, Tom. It's not up to the FBI. Jenkins is supposed to get his marching orders from Walsh, not the other way around."

So I kept calling Walsh. After a while my phone calls began to get shunted back to the switchboard and then around again in looping spirals all over the Justice Department. The words, "A Mr. Osborne's on the line," seemed to be enough to clear out the entire office.

One Friday I went to the U.S. Attorney's office in person, and as the receptionist darted off to collect excuses from her superiors as to why they couldn't see me, I copied down the number for Walsh's direct line off her desk. That got me through for a couple of calls, but then he got that number changed, and they began to shunt me around again.

Around this time I was watching a television show about missing children, hosted by a local columnist named Pete Monahan. Monahan is sort of Boston's answer to Jimmy Breslin or Mike Royko: the hard-hitting guy knuckling it up for the common man.

The next morning I put in a call to Monahan and told him about the runaround Walsh was giving me. So Monahan took my name and said he would make some calls and get back to me.

He never did, nor did he return my subsequent calls, but I would invoke him in my conversations with Walsh anyway and threaten to expose him and his boss to the media.

Walsh was unimpressed. "Look, Tom, I've been patient with you, but I'm getting a little tired of this harrassment. I'll call when Mr. Thorpe has made his decision. It's out of my hands."

All right then, I figured, if it's out of Walsh's hands then I'll build a fire under Thorpe. So I went to Uncle Henry to see if there was any old-boy network I might bring into play.

Uncle Henry was by now a dwindling figure in his eyepatch and gardening clothes. He'd retired from his firm under pressure from his board, and in his dotage he'd acquired a kind of distant sweetness. His own world had fallen apart in a cruel way, and gone was the grand bull who used to preside at the dinner table and shake his fist at the traffic in Alden harbor.

I found him pruning some shrubs on the windy lawn, cursing the thorns that penetrated his gray gardening gloves. He was pleased to be interrupted and served me one of his Bloody Marys out on the bench on the terrace as I raged about everyone's failure to come to my assistance.

"You're approaching this like some poor bastard off the boat," he said finally, with the old color rising in his neck. "Goddamn it, Tom, I promise you—you're going to get the kids back by Christmas. Barbara can't hold out much longer. She hasn't got the resources. She's got to come up for air.

"Now then," he said, clapping me on the knee and warming to his paternalism, "I know this fellow Thorpe. Upton Taylor at P. O. & L. went to school with him. Tell Upton to give Thorpe a call. Set a fire under the son of a bitch. Don't let yourself get lost in the shuffle."

I downed my Bloody Mary and stared into the old man's face for a moment. "All right, Uncle Henry," I said, setting down my glass. "I'll get back on the horse."

"That's the spirit," he said, rising a little painfully from the bench.

"No more whining. By Christmas," he called out as I hurried down the driveway. "By Christmas we'll all be singing goddamn carols together."

For the first time in a couple of weeks I found myself back on the phone with Hill.

"Look, Tom," said Hill. "I've heard from this fellow Walsh."

"You have?"

"Yes, and I have to say he's very upset with you. He wants you to stop calling him. He says he'll deal with me but not with you."

"Is that all he told you? Didn't he give any indication about the UFAP warrant?"

"Tom, I've said it before. I really think you're in the wrong court here. You've gone off on your own tangent with this thing and look where it's gotten you."

"Look, Peter," I said. "I don't need you to scold me or to stick up for their side. I need your help. You've got a partner in your firm named Upton Taylor."

Hill sighed. "Yes, Tom. Upton's a senior partner here."

"Well, I understand he was Thorpe's school chum or something. I want you to get him on the phone to Thorpe and find out what the hell is going on."

"I don't know if I can really ask a senior partner—"

"You can do this for me," I said. "You can get on the phone, and tell Uppity or whatever his name is to make a phone call, can't you?"

There was a long pause, and Hill sniffed slightly. "Very well, Tom," he said. "But I think you're barking up the wrong tree."

"I don't feel good about this, Tom," Yantorno said about the delay. "Maybe Hill's right. They're taking too damn long. They won't commit themselves. I just don't think they're taking your problem very seriously. And I don't think it starts with Thorpe. I think it starts with the Attorney General and the director of the FBI. They don't want their people tangled up in this stuff."

"Well, don't give up yet, Rick," I told him. "I've got a connection to Thorpe's office. Old school tie. And Barker at the state police— he's putting the pressure on, too. Walsh could still come through."

"Well, Tom," said Yantorno doubtfully. "I hope you're right."

As if to confirm that I was right, Hill called that same day to tell me that Upton had indeed been on the phone to his former roommate and that Thorpe had heard of my case and described himself as "not disinterested." Thorpe promised to call Upton as soon as he'd had a chance to confer with Walsh.

I was jubilant. Now I was getting somewhere. The connections were paying off.

On the 24th of October, Flynn came by to tell me that he had called Mary Ramirez in the missing-persons unit of the state police.

"Did she have anything?"

"Tom," Flynn said gently. "I wouldn't pin any hopes on them. I can never get them on the phone. I've tried a dozen times in the past four weeks, and I still haven't spoken once to Ramirez. But I've called around and everybody tells me not to bother. All this missing-persons unit is is a couple of cops and a Rolodex."

"But Barker said—"

"They don't investigate anything, Tom. They're just a clearinghouse in case somebody turns up at a school or something. I'm not even sure there *is* a Mary Ramirez."

A couple of days passed, and I began to call the U.S. Attorney's office again, but nobody would put me through any longer, and if I got as far as Walsh's or Thorpe's secretary I would be sweetly told that the boss was out: out of the office, out of the state, out of the country.

In the meantime Susan had gotten in touch with a slick outfit in Houston, Texas, called LostSearch that specialized in searching for children who'd been abducted overseas. At her urging I talked to a very smooth, eager young executive named David Chandler who sounded to me like a salesman for high-tech equipment.

Chandler said he handled this kind of case all the time; it was his business. He said he could handle Israel. He'd make a phone call to clarify the legal situation, but traditionally he didn't handle these situations through the courts. He told me he would send me a contract, and after I'd had a chance to check out his prices I could come out to Houston for an interview, and he could get to work.

But I was kind of dubious about Chandler. He was moving a little too fast for me at that point because I hadn't yet framed the problem in terms of getting the kids out. I was still trying to find out where they were. I didn't want some heavy-handed private dick kidnapping my children on my behalf. If we were going that route, I had to retrieve them myself.

The price Chandler was asking turned out to be two or three thousand dollars start-up money and additional charges by the hour up to around ten thousand dollars. It seemed that everybody who was upbeat about doing something always wanted a lot of dough. Money wasn't a sticking point for me, but it did cast doubt on everybody's assurances. So I decided to stall Chandler at least until I'd heard from Thorpe.

Finally, on the afternoon of October 28th, Hill called to relay Upton Taylor's report on his conversation with Thorpe.

"They've come to a decision, Tom," he said.

At last, I thought, waving Susan to my side in the kitchen. "Are they going to come through with the warrant?"

"Well," said Hill, "let me just take you right through my notes here. Let's see. Mr. Thorpe evidently told Upton that the FBI is of the view that if your ex-wife is in Israel as suspected, it isn't appropriate to issue a UFAP warrant from the U.S. Attorney's office."

"What?" I said, as Susan stared quizzically at me. "Why the hell not?"

"I think he explains himself, Tom. Just allow me to continue," said Hill. "Upton says that Mr. Thorpe thought you should consult with the district attorney's office—I guess he means in Hammond—and request the issuance of a provisional arrest warrant against Mrs. Osborne."

"But we've *got* an arrest warrant, for Christ's sake."

Susan sat on the stool beside me and stared into her lap.

"Yes," said Hill. "Yes, I suppose you do. But to continue, Tom—Mr. Thorpe says the district attorney's office should seek information about her from the Office of International Affairs. He pointed out that a UFAP warrant should only be issued if it is determined that Mrs. Osborne is in Boston."

"In Boston?"

"That's right."

"But how can they issue a UFAP if she's still in the state?"

"I don't know, Tom," said Hill. "Maybe he's saying he can't take this on if it's outside his jurisdiction."

"But he's a federal prosecutor, Peter. That's the whole point of going for a UFAP."

"Look, Tom," said Hill. "You're asking me to interpret a memo of a telephone call. You want me to tell you the rest?"

"All right," I said.

"All right," Hill said with a sniff. "Mr. Thorpe said that Mr. Walsh told him that you'd asked the FBI to do five things, which Mr. Thorpe suggested should be directed to the district attorney's office instead."

"What?" I said, and realized I was glaring at Susan, as if she were a surrogate for Hill. I promptly closed my eyes tight.

"These five things are: request information, conduct a computer check, request the Colorado state police to interview Barbara's parents, check telephone toll records, and interview the rabbi."

I opened my eyes again. "Interview the rabbi? Damn it, Peter, that's not it. I don't need any of that stuff. I just want them to call the embassy in Tel Aviv. If the embassy would talk to me *I'd* make the call. But everyone says this has got to be a government-to-government thing, and all I want is a couple of hours' legwork out of these sons of bitches so I can go get my kids."

"Yes, well," said Hill. "To continue: Mr. Thorpe suggested that after the district attorney's office has tried to do these five things I should telephone Walsh to discuss the matter. Mr. Thorpe also suggested that future telephone calls made to the FBI or the U.S. Attorney's office be made by me, not by you."

"Oh Christ," I said, sitting down beside Susan and rubbing my eyes.

"He was very adamant about that, Tom. They don't want you calling them all the time. They only want to deal with me."

I couldn't talk for a few seconds as Susan reached over and touched my hand.

"Tom?" asked Hill. "Are you there?"

"Yes," I said.

"Well, Tom? Now do you understand?"

"Understand what? Understand that it's complete bullshit?"

"No, Tom," said Hill sternly. "Do you understand why they can't help you?"

"Because they don't want to do anything," I began to say, but then it finally hit me. I'd become an embarrassment to Hill. He was making excuses for them. It was almost as if Hill was on their side.

I hung up the phone and felt for a moment as though a door had swung into me. I thought of great-granduncle Louis Osborne's portrait on the wall outside Hill's office. These contacts of mine, these connections, these old-school pals: they were just bonds entangling me in a system that had no intention of helping me.

This was their system I was dealing with—Hill's, Walsh's, Jenkins's, Thorpe's. They were bound to protect it. How could I have believed they were going to help me?

14

THE LETTER

In the mail that Saturday was a letter from Walsh confirming Thorpe's report. It's four years later, and I still can't read it with anything approaching equanimity, but since it expresses all the ambivalence, contradiction, and evasion of the Justice Department's policy on parental abduction, maybe it should be digested a little at a time.

October 25, 1983

Re: Barbara Osborne

Dear Mr. Yantorno:

We are unable to authorize the issuance of a UFAP warrant for Barbara Osborne on the basis of the information presently available because that information fails to disclose evidence of international or interstate travel. . . .

This, of course, was nonsense. According to the present and former Assistant U.S. Attorneys I've since consulted, Yantorno had in fact presented Walsh with overwhelming evidence of international travel.

Barbara's note, with its "I've taken the children," "no truce" and "we'll be traveling from time to time," was in itself compelling evidence of interstate flight. Combined with her history of instability, her secret applications for passports for the children in August, her threats to take the children to Israel, her references to Marcus, her phony address on Brisby Street, her standing order at the storage

127

company to send her effects to Israel, and the inability of state and local police to find any trace of her in Massachusetts, the note was like icing on the cake. A fraction of such evidence would have been sufficient had the UFAP warrant been requested on a fugitive suspected of bank robbery or terrorism.

In fact, a UFAP warrant generally requires very little evidence because, as Yantorno said, it's never actually prosecuted.* So the federal magistrates and judges who grant UFAP warrants—many of them former federal prosecutors themselves—tend not to scrutinize UFAP warrant applications as carefully as they might a request for a federal kidnapping warrant because their issuance of a UFAP warrant is extremely unlikely to be subject to review by another court.

Thousands of federal crimes are committed every week that are never prosecuted by the Justice Department, and one of the functions of U.S. Attorneys is to decide which cases to accept. In this decision they are guided not only by the statutes, but also by the Justice Department guidelines laid down in the U.S. Attorney's manual. These guidelines not only define the Justice Department's policy on various crimes; they also validate federal prosecutors' discretion to decline any case they may deem too ungainly, untimely, controversial, flimsy, expensive, or labor-intensive to be worth their while.

As far as the Justice Department was concerned in 1983, parental abduction fit all of those bills. In many cases it was difficult for federal prosecutors, some of them refugees from their own divorces and custody battles, to satisfy themselves that the custodial parent was in the right, whatever the custody decree may have originally stipulated. For all they knew custody may have been assigned to a parent who was only marginally and perhaps temporarily more competent. The custodial parent may have since become neglectful or abusive, or married someone neglectful or abusive. How was a prosecutor to know whether the abducting parent had in fact rescued a child from abuse?

Even assistant U.S. Attorneys who convince themselves of the merits of particular parental abduction cases sense from their anguished contacts with distraught parents that if they accept a case they will be submitting themselves to meddlesome private investigators, elaborate and expensive extradition proceedings, and innumerable phone calls from custodial parents like me demanding action prosecutors can't initiate and information they can't obtain.

The sticky, grubby complexity of parental abduction is forbidding enough, but the scale of it is staggering. If, as some parent groups were claiming, there are from 25,000 to 750,000 parental abductions a year, how could an already overburdened Justice Department be expected to take them on? In 1983 FBI Director William Webster warned Congress that if it forced the FBI to act on every parental kidnapping case that came over the transom, its agents would be unable to process UFAP warrant applications in priority cases of murder, robbery, and terrorism.

I don't know if the FBI actually believed the parent groups' figures or just embraced them to validate its own reluctance to involve itself in what many in the law-enforcement community preferred to regard as a civil matter: an aggravated violation of a custody decree. Even in the face of congressional efforts to force it into parental abduction cases, the Justice Department was recalcitrant, even defiant.

The UFAP statute had never excluded parental abduction nor even attached special evidentiary requirements. But in the U.S. Attorney's manual, the Justice Department maintained that Congress intended, in spite of itself, to include parental abduction in the UFAP statute only if the child's life was in danger. Assistant U.S. Attorneys were therefore instructed to enforce a strictly physical definition of endangerment and generally to disregard evidence of the kind of psychological damage and indirect hazard I was prepared to demonstrate.

D.A.'s like Yantorno therefore would have had to provide the U.S. Attorney with reports from social agencies demonstrating past physical abuse by abducting parents, or direct testimony that children were currently being physically abused or threatened. The Catch-22 for Yantorno and Flynn, of course, was that without a UFAP warrant and FBI assistance in locating Ben and Sara, they had no way of obtaining testimony of continuing abuse.

After considerable lobbying by parent groups, Congress passed the Parental Kidnapping Act of 1980, which sought to exclude the endangerment requirement by specifically including parental abduction cases in the UFAP statute. But it turned out not to have been specific enough because the Justice Department continued for two more years to insist that Congress really meant to require evidence of endangerment and instructed its field offices accordingly.

In February of 1983, Congress added language specifically excluding any need to demonstrate endangerment in applying for UFAP warrants in parental kidnapping cases. In addition, it required the Justice Department to report to Congress every six months the number of UFAP warrant applications for parental kidnapping cases it has processed.*

And so, on October 25th, 1983, the date of Walsh's letter to Yantorno, the U.S. Attorney could decline my case only by effectively raising the standards of evidence out of Yantorno's reach.

The letter then went on to discuss extradition.

> Although Mr. Osborne believes that his wife may have taken the children to Israel, the appropriate remedy in such a case would be extradition or deportation. As you know, the request for extradition must come directly from the District Attorney's office to the Office of International Affairs of the Department of Justice. I have spoken to John Hooks of that office who tells me that if the offense is extraditable under applicable treaties, Justice will forward the request to the State Department provided you can establish that the fugitive is present in Israel and provided you are willing to pay the substantial expenses of extradition (including translation). . . .

Of course, getting the federal government to assist in establishing that Barbara was in Israel was the main purpose of our request for a UFAP warrant in the first place. So in effect the feds were insisting on information from Yantorno that only the feds themselves could have provided with a simple phone call to Israel.

The complexity of the extradition process evidently depends on the legal system of the corresponding country. For instance, the United States can extradite a fugitive from France, which is a fellow code-law country, almost as easily and inexpensively as New York might extradite a fugitive from California.

But extradition from a common-law country like Israel is more elaborate, involving a time-consuming flow of certified documents and correspondence, and expensive and cumbersome translations and travel arrangements, the cost of which Yantorno's office would have to absorb.

But it turns out that the denial of the UFAP warrant itself had turned extradition into a dead issue. What John Hooks may have failed to tell Walsh, and in any case what Walsh and Hooks failed to tell either Yantorno or me, was that Hooks had never pursued extradition in a parental abduction case, as he still has not, up to the time of this writing, because parental abduction had been specifically excluded by the United States itself in every extradition treaty to which it's a signatory. Thus by denying a UFAP warrant, which would have created a basis for extradition distinct from the state felony charge of parental abduction, Walsh had effectively eliminated any possibility of Barbara's extradition from Israel.

Extradition, of course, would only return Mrs. Osborne to the United States, not the children. . . .

This was nonsense, too, of course, except insofar as a UFAP warrant in a bank robbery case would facilitate the capture of the robber and not necessarily the recovery of his loot. At the very least, Barbara's extradition would have cleared the way for my claiming immediate custody of the children in Israel.

I guess it's at this point in Walsh's letter that the question of the efficacy of the criminalization of parental abduction rears its puzzled head. As a State Department official once told me, "The real object of criminalization of parental abduction in many states is as much to deter such abductions and to exert a kind of pressure that will result in the return of the child as to punish the abducting parent."*

But what I wanted to ask Walsh and Thorpe and all the rest of them was how anyone was going to help the parents of abducted children if there wasn't some kind of reciprocity. The law's attitude seemed to be, "Hey, we try to do what we can to bring a little order to these complicated family disputes, but what can we do when people act irresponsibly?"

My answer to that is that people are always going to act irresponsibly, but they're going to act even more irresponsibly if there's nothing standing in their way. There's got to be some kind of normative sanction, and what is the law if it isn't a repository for normative sanctions?

Walsh concluded with a few more helpful hints.

> I suggest, in the meantime, that you put the state kidnapping warrant into the NCIC [National Crime Information Computer] and that you ask INS [Immigration and Naturalization Service] and Customs to issue a stop notice on Mrs. Osborne, in case she attempts to reenter the United States. . . .

But here Walsh was once again recommending something that his UFAP warrant denial precluded. Flynn had already entered Barbara's name into the NCIC network, but it turned out that Yantorno could not enter Barbara's name into the U.S. customs computer that screens criminals trying to leave the country because customs would enter only the names of parental abductors on whom federal felony warrants had been issued.

> Of course, if you do uncover evidence of flight which would make FBI involvement appropriate, please let me know immediately.
>
> Very truly yours,
Stanley J. Thorpe
United States Attorney
>
> By Theodore E. Walsh
Assistant U.S. Attorney

For a couple of hours I went berserk, indulging a kind of mordant jubilation that they'd set all this bullshit down on paper. Now I had something to take to the press. Now I could finally expose these bastards for lying to me, for stalling me, for running me around in circles.

But it didn't take long for that to pass. Once I'd lifted my eyes a little I realized that exposing the American system of justice wasn't my purpose. All I wanted was my kids, and now nobody was going to help me find them.

Yantorno called me Saturday afternoon to commiserate.

"I'm sorry, Tom," he said. "I just don't know what those guys must be thinking."

"I don't believe it, Rick. It doesn't make sense."

"I don't either, Tom."

"It's bullshit. Insufficient evidence? What are they *talking* about?"

Yantorno was silent.

"They're telling me they can't get me the information unless I give them the information I need them to get."

"Yeah," said Yantorno. "That's hitting it on the head."

"Well," I said. "What about this extradition business? Is that what it's going to take to get them to make the call? Can you guys request that? I mean, is there still a chance they'll extradite her on a state warrant?"

"Well," said Yantorno with a sigh. "That's the thing, Tom. I wish I could say we could. But I called up this guy Hooks, and he says it's going to cost a lot, and we're going to have to pay for it."

"Who's we?"

"Us. The D.A.'s office."

"How much is it going to cost?"

"Thousands. There're airline tickets, fees, documents that need filling out, translations. . . ."

"Hell," I said. "Then *I'll* pay for it."

"No, Tom. I'm afraid it can't work that way. You can't purchase government services. It's got to come out of our budget.

"I've talked this thing over with the D.A., and we just can't see how we could afford it. I mean, you know how much we want to get her, Tom. I want you to get those kids, and I want to prosecute Barbara to the limit of the law. We've got the crime, we've got the evidence. It makes a hell of a good case. But we're talking thousands of dollars just to get her back here, not to mention a trial, and that would wipe us out. We just can't do it."

"Then who—"

"We think it should come out of their budget, Tom."

"Yeah, but they're not going to do anything—"

"Look, Tom, we're talking about the federal government here, the government of the most powerful country in the world. They can get her out of Israel if they want to. They can go to Israel and say, 'Look, friends, we're going after this criminal, and we don't expect you to help us, but we don't expect you to stop us either,' and they can get her. Why should the county pay for it? She's violated federal law here, Tom. The feds should pay for it."

"But they won't."

Yantorno sighed. "But they won't. Right."

"So what do we do?"

Yantorno paused. "I don't know, Tom. I would like to say I'm going to think of something, but unless she comes to the States I don't know what we can do. I've reached the end of the line here, Tom. I've run out of gambits."

"Then what do I do? Where does that leave me? They won't help. You can't help. Where the hell does that leave me?"

Yantorno was silent for a moment.

"Look, Rick," I said. "I'm sorry. I know you tried. I'm just too pissed off right now. I've got to hang up."

The short of it seemed to be that the Congress and the press and We the people were telling their law enforcement agencies to do something about missing kids. But they believed that they couldn't really do much of anything about it because it's too damn big. There was no way they were going to commit resources to chasing down kids. But if they had openly admitted that, they would have just drawn fire. So Walsh and Thorpe and Jenkins had gotten caught in this defensive posture, this pattern of evasion, and all they could do was spin my wheel.

15

THE WAKE

Up to this point I thought I'd been bugging all these bureaucrats because I'd believed they were going to help me. But now that they'd turned me down, I began to wonder if I'd launched my attack on the powers-that-be just to give me the sensation of doing something.

My life had become strangely compartmentalized. I'd been taking five courses toward my doctorate and dividing the day into three parts. I would make my first battery of phone calls in the morning and then wolf down a tuna sandwich around noon and drive in for my classes. I usually returned home in the afternoon for more phone calls and then studied all evening with tremendous concentration, going into a kind of trance, like some Buddhist monk. Finally, from ten at night to one in the morning, Susan and I made our moonstruck plans for the following day.

I could sustain this routine of classes and phone calls, plots and ploys only so long as I believed that progress was being made, that my agents were closing in on Barbara. But now that I'd run out of agents it seemed intolerable that I should go on pursuing my doctorate while my kids were in danger. After six weeks of not being able to get one of the most prestigious law firms in Boston to figure out what the law was, six weeks of getting nothing but runarounds from the FBI and the U.S. Attorney as my children's tracks disappeared in the sand, I began to lose faith in everything.

I considered flying off to Israel and standing on a street corner, handing out pictures of the kids. I imagined kidnapping Dan Rather.

I fantasized chaining myself to the door of the Justice Department.
I envisioned bursting into Empress Gems and grabbing those guys
by the throat.

I'd tell myself, *Wait a minute, Osborne. You're not Clint Eastwood. You don't beat up on people.*

But then I'd say, *What the hell do you mean you're not Clint
Eastwood? These are your children. Get a gun. Get a bomb. Get on
a plane. Pistol-whip these bastards into doing something.*

Through all this the only person I could depend upon was Susan.
She'd become perhaps even more swept into the game than I was,
because she hadn't been drawn into the evolution of the crisis. She
hardly knew Barbara, so on the one hand she could give her the
benefit of the doubt, while on the other hand Barbara was simply a
woman who had taken my children: a player to be outwitted and
overcome.

I still don't know where Susan found the courage to stick by me.
We weren't even married, and compounding everything was not only
Alden's but the Osborne family's conservatism. Our living together
troubled my family, and we were urged to marry immediately, for
the sake of propriety, but we thought it would be unfair to the kids.
We weren't going to present them with any *fait accomplis* in that
department.

Susan had to believe in so much at once: not only in herself but in
me and in the kids. And she had to believe that the children belonged
with me and with her, that we should all be a part of her future. By
keeping me from imploding, Susan's belief in me was self-fulfilling.

When I raged about the U.S. Attorney and the FBI and the State
Police and all the rest of it, she always helped me keep the situation
in focus. She told me to conserve myself and my resources for the
time when I found out where Ben and Sara were. We could only act
when we knew something, and we still didn't even know for sure if
they were in Israel. I wasn't going to be any use to them if I let
Barbara drive me crazy.

Every now and then I would reread Barbara's letter, hoping I might
have missed some clue or hidden message. But on its face it offered
so little reassurance, and between the lines it was ominous.

No truce . . . No choice . . . We will be traveling from time to time. I had tried to believe that she would be in touch "often enough," as she'd promised, "when I can and where I can." I couldn't believe Barbara would be so cruel as not to tell me how the kids were doing. As the weeks turned to months, I became more convinced that something terrible had happened: they hadn't made it to Israel after all, they were in Argentina, they were in Uganda, they'd all gotten sold to some Saudi, they were dead.

I entered into a bizarre period of vagrant episodes that I seemed to bump into like a sleepwalker.

Shopping for groceries one evening, I was approached by a neighbor of mine who was a lawyer.

"Tom," he said, taking me aside by the dairy case. "I've heard from your uncle about your difficulty, and I wonder if you would mind my giving you a little advice."

"No," I said. "I can use all the help I can get."

"Good, Tom. What I wanted to suggest to you," he said, lowering his voice, "is that you effect your own death."

"Effect my own death? What do you mean—kill myself?"

"No, no," he said. "Seriously, Tom. I know it sounds odd, but as I understand it, Barbara's running out of money, isn't she?"

"Well, yeah," I said.

"So my advice is that you effect your own death, see? Susan calls up and gets your obituary printed in the *Globe*, and then you send a copy off to Barbara's parents. See what I mean? Barbara will figure you're dead and the coast is clear and she'll come forward to claim your children's inheritance and—bango—you have her arrested."

"Great idea," I told him.

"Well," he said, "I'm just glad I could be of—"

"No, really," I said. "Thanks a lot. Effect my own death. That would be a terrific thing to do, wouldn't it? That would be a wonderful thing to do to my children."

"Never mind, then," he said with a wounded look, shoving his cart down the aisle. "I was only trying to help."

One morning I was bleakly watching the local news when Governor Dukakis and none other than U.S. Attorney Stanley Thorpe announced that they were setting up a two-million-dollar joint task force to deal with the stolen car problem.

I couldn't stand the sight of them grinning at each other, and I switched off the set and rushed into the kitchen.

"Goddamn it," I told Susan. "They won't even make a phone call for my kidnapped children, and now they're going to blow two million dollars on stolen cars? What the hell is wrong with this country?"

Susan suggested that I write a letter to the *Globe*. But the letter kept me whipped up for days and became a repository for all my anger and frustration. Choice phrases would occur to me in class, at lunch, in the bathroom.

Driving home from work one afternoon I became so inspired that I swerved off the highway to write down a few more telling lines when a state trooper stopped to ask if anything was the matter.

"No, Officer," I heard myself say. "Nothing's the matter. Anything the matter with you?"

I could feel the hairs stand up on the back of my neck as he scowled at me. I wanted to grab him by the collar and hurl him into the highway. What was he doing out there, chasing speeders on the highway, when he could have been searching for my children?

"Then move along, sir," he finally said, adjusting his shades and returning to his cruiser.

"Thank you, Officer," I called out after him, tossing him the bone.

The international news was full of bombs going off in Beirut and Palestinians rioting along the West Bank. And the local news was full of missing persons: an amnesiac father of four was returned to his family in a bewildering blaze of television lights, a stolen baby was recovered at the Mexican border.

But the story I remember best from this period concerned a trucker out West somewhere whose children had been missing for five years. And for those five years he had faithfully set presents out for his children every Christmas and waited for them by the tree.

Only two months before, when I still believed in my connections, I wouldn't have identified with him. I would have felt sorry for him, but I would have figured he simply didn't have the resources to locate his children. He didn't know what buttons to push, what calls to make, what old school chums to call upon.

But now I knew better. He and I were adrift together, and I thought of the birthday cakes still awaiting Ben and Sara in the freezer, the birthday presents gathering dust on the closet shelf, and I sat with Susan and cried.

One night as I was doing the dishes the phone rang, and it was Kitty, Barbara's mother, asking if we'd heard anything.

"No, Kitty," I said. "How about you?"

"No, nothing," she said quickly. "Not a thing. I'm worried, Tom. Have you been able to find out anything?"

"Nothing," I said.

"You don't have any idea where they are?"

I wasn't going to tell her that I suspected they were in Israel, because if that was where Barbara was hiding I didn't want Kitty alerting her, so I said, "No I don't, Kitty. Do you have any theories?"

"Well, Tom," she said. "I think they may be in Canada."

"Canada? Is that right?"

"Yes," said Kitty. "I seem to recall her mentioning that she'd always wanted to live in Canada."

"That's interesting," I said.

"She always had this thing for Montreal."

"Well, what would you suggest I do?"

"I don't know," she said. "Have you thought of the Mounties maybe? Or maybe Interpol?"

"I never thought of that," I said. "But I know what I'll do first. I'll run a computer check through the school system."

Kitty paused a moment. "You can do that?"

"Yes," I said confidently. "Every school child in every Western country is logged on a computer. I'll just have the kids' names chased down and get back to you."

"Ah," she said. "I see."

"Well, thanks for the tip," I said. "I'll be in touch."

By now I was convinced that Kitty knew exactly where the children were and was just fishing on Barbara's behalf. In my heart I still believed that Kitty didn't care, that she was lying to us, trying to throw us off the scent. But after I hung up I wondered if Kitty might have been on the level. Maybe Barbara *was* in Canada. Or maybe she was back in Colorado. Maybe Kitty couldn't take the heat any-more. Maybe she was scared and wanted out. Maybe Kitty was sick of Barbara the way she always got sick of Barbara, and she'd called to give us a sign.

Susan and I decided we couldn't afford to ignore the possibility that she was trying to tell us something. So we called information in Montreal and found a new listing for a B. Kaye, but "B" turned out to be an indignant old man named Bertram. Susan called information in several neighboring towns, but she came up empty, and in the meantime the Mounties were no more animated by my tale of woe than their American counterparts. We called information in Colorado as well, and even found someone in the state education department who agreed to check his computer records to see if Ben and Sara were registered anywhere. But after a day or so we dismissed the Canadian scenario.

I made calls to Senator Kennedy and to Senator Paula Hawkins, who was evidently sponsoring legislation that would make parental ab-duction a federal crime, and I called a lot of other legislators too, but all I would get would be some junior staffer telling me to write a letter.

I tried, but by now it seemed so beside the point, so removed from the pain I was feeling. What did Edward Kennedy or Paula Hawkins or the Ninety-sixth Congress have to do with Ben and Sara?

Susan reminded me, however, that I couldn't kiss off the entire U.S. government. No matter what I did, I was going to need new passports for the kids.

So I called the State Department in Washington and was shunted over to Gerry Miller, a paralegal in the Office of Citizenship Appeals and Legal Assistance.

I told him the whole story and asked if he could provide me with a second set of passports for Ben and Sara. He said that if he'd been given a court order preventing Barbara from taking the children out of the country he could have denied them passports. But now that they'd been issued it wasn't within his power to revoke them, or grant me a second set.

"Unless we're notified otherwise and in advance, Mr. Osborne," he said, "our office has to assume joint custody. That's the natural state of affairs. Either parent can apply for a passport."

"You mean there isn't any law requiring the signature of the custodial parents?"

"No," he said. "It's in there. It stipulates that the application must be executed by a parent or guardian of the minor or a person *in loco parentis.*"

"But why doesn't it call for a custodial parent's signature on the application?"

"I don't know if you understand what I mean," he said. "The passport application itself may not say anything about being a custodial parent, but it's in the regulation."

"Look," I said. "Did she or did she not apply under false pretenses?"

"Well," he said, "she violated the court order. But she would not be violating our regulations because they assume by default that she's got the right."

By this time I did not have the energy to ask how parents were supposed to know that they had to be a custodial parent when they applied for their children's passports if it didn't say so on the application, or how it could be that she hadn't violated their regulations simply because the State Department didn't have a copy of the court order.

"What I can do, though, Mr. Osborne," Miller said, "is flag little Ben and Sara's names in the computer so that next time your wife applies for passports for them we'll be notified."

I began to perk up. "And you'll notify me?"

"That's right. If she does apply we would call you, and you could let us know whether you want us to grant them new passports."

"So you would deny them passports?"

"We'd need a court order for that."

"I've got a court order."

"Then yes, we could deny issuance, and you'd be given a copy of her application."

"That would be great," I said. "Let's do that."

"But of course we couldn't deny issuance if she applied for them in a foreign country."

"Why not?"

"Well, because then the law of the host country applies. You'd have to get a court order from the host country for us to deny issuance."

"But could you still notify me?"

"Oh sure," Miller said. "Why don't you give me your address and I'll let you know when she applies next time."

As I gave Miller my address, it occurred to me to ask, "But what's the life of my children's passports?"

"Uh, it's five years up to the age of eighteen. When were they issued?"

"In August."

"So they won't expire until—"

"—1988."

"1988. That's right. But you've got to realize, Mr. Osborne," he said, "these things do drag on sometimes."

On Thursday, November 3rd, I came home late from class to find Susan waiting for me on the doorstep with a stricken look.

It kept falling to her to be the bearer of bad news, but I had never seen her look so troubled, sitting and hugging her knees in the evening chill, and I thought, *Oh God, she's heard something.*

"It's the kids," I said. "Something's happened to the kids."

But she looked up at me and shook her head. "No," she said weakly. "It's your Uncle Henry, Tom. He's just died."

I don't know if I can describe the mixture of feelings I had as I stumbled around Uncle Henry's Peaceable Kingdom that night. I grieved for Uncle Henry as I walked the cobble beach, but I also grieved for my children and for myself, my fatherhood. I was so tired of people disappearing on me. The center of the family had given way, and I wanted to chase after Uncle Henry and shout, "Wait a minute, old man. Where are you going? You were going to find my kids, remember? You were going to bring them back for Christmas."

The family scattered his ashes off the beach and gathered in the main house for a wake. The concern at the wake was how Aunt Jane would spend her first widow's Christmas, and a conspiracy of my cousins arranged for the family to gather at the Osborne house in Boston. Beyond this nucleus others of my family wandered, trading stories.

Uncle Henry was dead, and with him had died all his reassurances. I was by this time so obsessed by my children's abduction that I couldn't leave my tragedy at the door to Aunt Jane's. I spent the day circulating among my cousins, reading the interminable letter I was still composing for the *Globe*.

Susan could do little to stop me as I downed memorial Bloody Marys and wandered through the room with my tattered letter. The letter was almost incoherent with impotent rage, but I read it like Scripture, glaring at any cousin who dared shrink away for refreshment.

In the afternoon a couple of late arrivals who hadn't heard about my difficulties innocently asked after the kids.

I told them about the kids and about the D.A. and the FBI and the U.S. Attorney, until I'd backed them into a corner and was reading to them from the letter.

" 'Eight weeks ago my six- and seven-year-old children were abducted,' " I read. " 'I miss them. I worry about them. And I can't get help from the authorities to find them. Why not take one federal and one state law enforcement officer away from the new task force on stolen cars and assign them to help find stolen kids? Maybe a few cars won't get found, but maybe a few kids will get back where they belong.' "

Susan approached and tried to draw me aside, but I shook her off and continued to read, my voice rising until the rest of the gathering had fallen silent, and suddenly I caught sight of my cousin Bob and I realized what I'd done. The family had gathered to honor Uncle Henry but I could only perceive this monumental loss through the prism of my own bereavement.

Susan and my cousin Bob quietly led me off into the kitchen.

"I'm sorry," I said, touching Bob's shoulder.

"That's all right," he said as the kitchen door swung closed behind us.

"Your father's dead," I told him, "and I pull a stunt like this."

Bob sighed and smiled. "So you're an asshole," he said gently. "What else is new?"

Susan smiled and patted my arm.

"Look, Tom," Bob said, sitting near me as caterers bustled by. "No offense to the might and majesty of Patridge Osborne and Whoever, but I know this lawyer in town named Kugler. Real aggressive guy. Very able. I don't know if he deals in this sort of stuff or not, and he's real busy, but why don't you give him a call?"

Bob was almost a decade younger than I, but now he was suddenly taking on his father's paternalistic role: looking past his own grief and thinking about me.

"Another lawyer," I said.

"Well, yeah, another lawyer," he said. "But not just any other lawyer. This guy's very creative, very unorthodox. I should know. He ate my lawyer for breakfast last week."

Susan and I looked at each other for a moment and shrugged.

"All right, Bob," I sighed, drawing a pen from my jacket. "What's his number?"

16

SID

Early on the morning of Tuesday, November 8th, Andy Flynn drove out to the house. Of all the people we supposedly had working on this problem, he had seemed the least likely. But in the end he'd turned out to be the most helpful. He was always on the case, always willing to try things.

This particular morning he came in to report that the Israeli consulate had just told him about an Israeli cop in New York named Ripkin who acted as a kind of interface with American law enforcement.

"Then let's call him," I said, leading Andy to the phone. "Ask him about arrival times. Maybe he can get us what we need."

So Flynn put in a call and immediately got through to Ripkin, who said, "No problem. I'll get back to you with the information in twenty-four hours."

And sure enough, on Wednesday, November 9th, Ripkin called back to report that Barbara and the kids had arrived in Israel on September 13th and upon entry had given 445/3 Padkin Street, Hadera, as her Israeli address.

I couldn't believe it. Here was information I'd been spending months trying to get, and this cop comes through with it in twenty-four hours.

I shook Flynn's hand, and I rejoiced, of course, but mixed in with my elation was this intense anger, because surely someone along the way—the state police, the D.A., the FBI, the U.S. Attorney, the State Department—*someone* must have known about Ripkin. He could have answered all the questions I was trying to get them to answer. Why in hell hadn't they told me about him? I wouldn't have needed a kidnapping warrant or a UFAP or any of that bullshit. All they would have had to do was call this guy and get the information. But they wouldn't do it.

For the first time in eight weeks I began to get some focus on the kids again. They stopped being mere vacancies in my universe or fading snapshot icons on my bureau. Now I knew they were out there somewhere, breathing, moving, surviving.

I called Jean Stein at the Israeli consulate and asked if she knew what Hadera was like. She told me she had an aunt who lived in Hadera and remembered Padkin Street as a neighborhood of exclusive apartment buildings on the east side, within a couple of blocks of a nice school.

I shut my eyes and tried to envision them as positively as I could—those small, pale redheads in the strong Israeli sun, traipsing off to school in khaki clothes, carrying olive book bags as the neighborhood children fell into step alongside them. I imagined them eating austere meals at the school, Ben wrestling with mathematics in one corner of a school room, Sara leading the girls around the playground, Mag puzzling over Scripture, and Barbara keeping her vigil in the apartment as the money ran out.

And yet the address could have been a ruse to put everyone off the scent. I may have been pretty certain she was in Israel now, but I wasn't sure where.

Up to that point Susan and I had been too demoralized to call Sidney Kugler, the lawyer my cousin Bob had recommended. But Ripkin's information was like a shot of pure adrenalin, and on Friday, November 19th, I finally called Kugler and began to explain my situation.

"Look, Tom," he said. "Can I call you Tom? I can't talk right now. I'm busy. This is a busy time for me."

I sighed, figuring I'd racked up yet another brushoff. "Yeah, right," I said. "I understand. I'm sorry I—"

"So you better come in tomorrow."

"Tomorrow?" I said. "But tomorrow's Saturday."

"What's the matter? You can't come in on a Saturday?"

"Uh, no," I said. "That will be fine."

"Good," said Kugler. "Come in at eight. I'll leave word with security."

Kugler and Associates was on Tremont Street, in a new building overlooking the Boston Public Library. The outer lobby was all oak and granite and hanging plants, but Kugler himself worked in what could have been a mock-up for a small-town attorney's office, circa 1952. Battered gray filing cabinets were lined up along two walls, their drawers overflowing with bulging folders, and Kugler's unprepossessing steel desk was a jumble of memos, files, law journals, and papers. Degrees from Brandeis and Columbia hung on the walls, and the only clear area surrounded Kugler's speakerphone: a Radio Shack model in tan plastic.

Kugler was a little older than I: a small, thin, agitated man in a tapered suit. He had a habit of running his hands through his thin brown hair, so that it stood up at various odd angles during the course of a conversation. An unlit cigarette bobbed from his lips as he greeted us.

"I never light up," he assured us, showing us to chairs.

I delivered an updated account of the kids' abduction and my futile adventures with the powers-that-be, glancing over at Kugler from time to time to catch him staring back at me with a restless glint in his eye, jotting an occasional note, tugging at his sideburn, sucking slightly on his teeth.

My account, including Susan's promptings from her journal, had become almost a set piece by now, but when I was done the old indignation at the U.S. Attorney came over me again.

"I can't get anybody to pay attention," I told Kugler. "They can't get away with this disinvolvement business," I said, leaning forward. "They're supposed to help me, and they won't do it. I want you to make them do it. Barbara's committed a crime. If it's the only way I've got to animate them, I want you to push for extradition."

Kugler toyed with a strand of hair for a moment and swiveled around to gaze out the window.

"Look," he said finally, turning back. "I know what a tough thing it is to find this out, Tom, but finding your kids just isn't an executive department job."

"Right," I said impatiently, folding my arms. "Fine." I didn't need another officer of the court defending these bastards to me.

"No, listen," said Kugler. "Those guys were doing what they're paid to do—take the information and turn people off. So what else is new?"

"But this is an international matter now, Mr. Kugler," I said wearily. "These guys are the only way I'm going to get—"

"Jerked around," Kugler cut in. "And call me Sid.

"Look," he said, suddenly slapping his desk and rising to his feet, "we can get extradition."

"We can?"

"Sure," said Sid. "No problem. In ten years, maybe twenty. You've got to understand—your problem doesn't have anything to do with UFAP warrants and extradition. A UFAP warrant? Extradition?" he said, raising his hands to shoulder level. "What is that? What does that have to do with getting back the kids? Don't start with treaties between nations. Start with your ex-wife," he said, pressing a fist against his stomach. "Start with the fight with your ex-wife, and we'll get somewhere."

"But there's this form," I said wanly, holding up a kit that someone in the extradition office at the Justice Department had sent Yantorno.

Sid stood behind his desk now like a speaker at a rostrum and held up his hand.

"Forms?" he said. "Forget forms. For two months they've been making you fill out forms. Fill out forms? What is that? *What is that?*" he said, gripping the back of his chair. "We're going to get on the phone. We're going to find the kids. We're going to do what we have to do. But we're not going to get anywhere with *forms.*"

He saw me slump a little as I dropped the kit on his desk.

"Look," he said, sitting down again. "You guys are crapped out. They've been beating up on you for two months. They've got you dancing to their tune. Well, *forget* them. Why not dance to our own tune for a change? You need somebody who isn't *this* close to the problem," he said, pressing a palm against his nose. "Do you see what I mean? Somebody who's got his brain on. And that's me. I'm a problem solver. I can make it happen. I find solutions. That's what I do best. So what I'm asking you to do is let me take some of the load off your backs.

"My job is to find your kids, not to do everybody's bidding through this horrendous regulatory bullshit. I've got to keep *you* straight. I'm representing *you*. Do you see what I mean?"

Susan and I looked at each other. Who was this gorilla? I was thinking. He seemed to be telling me that all this time I'd been flunking the most important test of my life. And yet somewhere beyond my resentment I felt something come alive again: an unfamiliar pang of hope.

"Look," he said, sweeping aside a stack of papers, "I don't know if you have a legal problem, but you certainly have a problem, and the problem is getting your kids back. Who knows?" he said, leaning forward and shrugging. "That may or may not involve the law. That's all right. I'm going to help you."

Sid glanced at Susan. "But I'm going to need your complete confidence," he said, shrugging his shoulders slightly, like a prize fighter loosening up. "I've been listening to you, and I've been listening to Susan, and everything you tell me adds up. You're not kooks. You're nice people. You're a good father who wants his kids back, who wants them safe. I can trust you. And that's good, because as it is I may have to call in every chip I've got. I'm going to have to risk my professional reputation calling people I have a stake in. I've got to have everything tied down to begin with because you can't run fast unless you've got your sneaks on tight. Do you see what I mean?"

Susan and I nodded back at him.

"A lot of these things can turn out to be pretty straightforward. But what you're going to be buying is not so much my legal expertise as my energy. I don't like to let cases get protracted. I don't want to wear families out in court. So what I'm going to try for is immediate solutions. Are you with me?"

"Yes," I said.

"Good," he said, digging a calendar out of his desk and slapping it down before him. "Now, I need a deadline."

"A deadline?"

"I work better with a deadline. Let's set a deadline for getting the kids back."

I looked at Susan.

"A deadline?" Susan mouthed back at me.

"How's one month?" he said, opening the calendar to December. "One month and we get the kids back. How does that sound?"

"It sounds wonderful," I said, beginning to relax for the first time in eight weeks.

"Okay," he said. "Let's try some things."

"Missing kids, missing kids," Sid muttered, rubbing his lower lip with a pencil. "Let's see. I just read about somebody," he said, leaning forward suddenly and sorting through the papers on his desk. "Somebody on the West Coast. An old detective who finds kids. 'The Heartbreak Detective,' " he said, flourishing a newspaper clipping. "Let's call him up."

Susan reached over and touched my hand as Sid dialed the detective's number and switched on the speakerphone.

A woman picked up the phone and said she was the answering service and that the detective wouldn't be in until Monday.

"That's unacceptable, I'm afraid," said Sid. "I'm calling long distance. We have to talk now or the whole case falls apart. How can I reach him?"

"I'm afraid he's at home, sir. He has asked not to be disturbed."

"No good. You're going to have to call him and tell him it's Attorney Kugler calling from Boston, and it's urgent."

Sid gave her his number and hung up, leaning back for a moment and crossing his arms.

"So now what?" I began to say, but Sid held up a finger and moved his lips as if he were counting to himself, and suddenly the phone rang.

"Yes, sir. Yes, I did," he said, reaching over to switch the speakerphone on again.

"—know you?" the detective was asking. "The girl said—"

"Here's the thing, sir," said Sid. "I got a client here, and he's in a hurry. He's the custodial parent, but a couple of months ago his ex-wife snatched the kids and took them to Israel, and her trail's getting cold. What should he do?"

There was a pause and an exhalation of breath on the other end. "He's gonna need an Israeli," the detective said finally. "American dicks are useless over there. He needs somebody who knows the lay of the land."

"Any suggestions?"

"No," said the detective. "Sorry. Never did any international stuff. You're gonna have to find somebody."

"Okay sir, thanks very much. Sorry I had to bother you. You've been very helpful."

"That's okay," said the detective, and Sid hung up.

Sid looked over at Susan and me. "How'm I doing?" he said, glancing at Susan. "Am I doing anything for you? I don't know if I'm doing anything or not," he said, tapping his pencil on his desk. "But I'm doing *something*, you know what I mean? Do you understand that? I'm getting started."

Sid was cheering me up.

"That diamond dealer," Sid said. "What's his name?"

"Marcus."

"Marcus. Yeah. Diamond dealers. Diamond dealers," he said, frowning. "Wait a minute. I went to camp with a guy who knew one of the big families. There are only twelve diamond families, you know. Hassidim. Very shrewd. Very tough."

Sid glanced at me and seemed to read my impatience. I'd found out that much at least from Donegan.

"But you know about that stuff," Sid said, frowning. "Let me give this guy a call."

He called information in New York, and in a minute or so he had reached his old camp buddy. "Hey, Saul, this is Sid Kugler. Remember me? Yeah, Camp Moosilauke. That's right. How you been?"

Sid swiveled around and faced the window while he and Saul caught up on the last thirty-five years for a while. In a pause in the conversation he swiveled back around to face us.

"Listen, Saul," he said. "I've got a problem I wonder if you can help me with. I got to know the name of this diamond dealer who seems to live part-time in Hadera. First name's Marcus. Maybe got something to do with—" Sid cupped his hand over the phone. "Was it 'Empress'?"

"Uh—yes," I said.

"Empress," said Sid. "Empress Gems. Yeah, that's right. I need his last name and address. Can you get that for me? Terrific. It's good talking to you. Give my best to the wife and kids. You got a wife and kids? Great. Good-bye."

Sid turned to me again and asked, "How'm I doing?"

"Great," I said. "You're doing great."

"But we're forgetting something," he said. "We've got to keep me going here, right?"

I was still too amazed by Sid to pick up his cue.

Sid looked pained. "What I'm trying to say," he told me, clearing his throat, "is that I'm going to need five thousand dollars."

I gulped and sat up in my chair. "Five thousand dollars?"

"Hear me out, Tom," he said, leaning forward and clasping his hands. "Do you know why people hate lawyers?" he asked.

"Don't get me started," I said.

"No, listen," he said. "It's because lawyers don't relate on a human level. They don't sit down with a client and say they can do this and this, and they can't do that.

"But I'm going to lay everything out. What I'm going to contribute is this sense I have that we've got to get back the kids. I've got lots of juices for kids. I know lawyers who don't even take their children's calls. They tell their secretaries, 'Have him call back.' *Have him call back?* What is that?" Sid said, slapping down his hand. "What did you *have* him for?"

"But the fee—"

"Money's only money, Tom," Sid said. "It's the currency of my engagement, but it's not my engagement. If it takes us a couple of weeks, and I maybe make out a thousand dollars, what's the difference? What matters to me is that I have good clients who like me and respect me and come back to me the next time they need help.

"Now most lawyers charge by the hour. And in a lot of cases that works fine. General Motors' regular diet is legal problems. You figure some hours are going to be worthless to GM, and some are going to be worth millions.

"But people like you are the worst because the system isn't designed for you. It's designed for GM and these monkey lawyers who charge a hundred bucks an hour.

"A guy like you doesn't care about my hours. You want my energy, my ideas. My legal knowledge is going to inform this whole process, but the main reason you need a lawyer is because nobody's going to take a call from somebody with a kooky story about conversions and lost children. They want to talk to a lawyer. They want to talk to me.

"So I'm going to charge you by the job, not by the hour," he said. "The only way I'd charge by the hour is if the kids showed up tomorrow. Then I'd charge you for today and give you back the rest. Are you following this so far?"

Susan and I nodded back.

"Now let me tell you what I'm *not* going to do," he said sternly. "I'm not going to go into this thing retrospectively. Do you understand that? I'm not going to go back for some showdown with the FBI or this potato-head detective. Not because I couldn't, but because none of that matters. It's history. I've got to keep you aimed forward because that's where the *kids* are.

"So," he said finally, nodding at us. "Do we have an understanding?"

Susan and I leaned toward each other. I could see the hope rising in Susan's eyes as she nodded to me, and I turned and smiled at Sid.

"All right," I said.

"Good," said Sid, beaming at me now and snapping his fingers. "Next thing is Israel. Israel. Jews. Jews. We need Jews."

He thought for a moment. "Okay," he said. "I know this guy, he's very Jewish. He's on the board at City College. His mother runs the B'nai Brith or something. He used to work here. He's a good kid. I'll call him."

Sid checked his Rolodex and dialed. "Hello, Max? Sid Kugler. How you doing? Look, Max, I've got a client with a problem. Give me the name of a lawyer in Israel. Jacob who? Abramson? Yeah? If you say he's good, he's good. After all, you've worked with the best, right? No," said Sid, winking back at us. "I mean me. That's right. Good. Okay, give me his number. Thanks, Max. I'll give him a call."

Within the next two minutes Sid had gotten Abramson on the speakerphone from Israel. At first Sid and Abramson talked politics: Sid asked about the Knesset, Abramson asked about Koch.

Finally Sid said, "Look, Mr. Abramson, here's the thing. I've got this client here, Tom Osborne. Very nice fellow, very well-nourished. Good family. He thinks his ex-wife has taken his kids to Israel."

"Does he have legal custody?" asked Abramson with a slight Polish accent.

"Yes," said Sid. "How would that stand up in Israel?"

I leaned toward the speakerphone. Here was the question I'd spent thousands of dollars trying to get Hill and Geva and the entire goddamn State Department to answer.

"They'd probably back him up," said Abramson without missing a beat. "They usually respect American judgments. But you don't want to roll the dice on a thing like this. The courts here are slow, especially when it comes to custody. The effect on the kids could be disastrous, and in the process what's to prevent the mother from taking off with them again?"

"Then what do we do?" I called out before Sid could respond.

"That's my client," Sid told Abramson. "I've got him on the speakerphone."

"How do you do, sir," said Abramson. "I'd suggest you avoid the courts. I'd suggest that if you've got the stomach for it we better set up an operation. Pick them up, get you and them out of the country."

"Can you help us?" asked Sid.

"Yes, that's not a problem," Abramson replied. "We've handled these things before. I'm coming to the States for some business in two weeks. Get me some information and some pictures. I have a detective who works with me. You got any guesses where she is?"

I gave him the Padkin Street address the Israeli liaison officer had given us.

"Okay," said Abramson. "My detective will check out this address. No matter where they turn out to be, he'll find the kids in a week."

"What's this going to cost?" said Sid.

Abramson thought for a moment. "The detective should be about three hundred dollars. We'll cost three thousand dollars. Maybe five if we wind up in court."

Sid switched off the speakerphone and looked at me. "What do you think?"

What did I think? I thought Sid and Abramson were gifts from God.

"Okay," I said.

"Okay," said Sid, switching on the phone again. "Agreed."

We arranged to meet with Abramson on December 2nd and Sid signed off.

"So," said Sid, "are we getting anywhere? Is this what you need?"

I had to laugh. I was beginning to think that Sid was the most effective human being I'd ever seen. In a little more than an hour he'd answered questions everyone else had failed to answer in ten weeks. Everything seemed to be rolling.

"Sid," I blurted, "you're fantastic."

"All right, good," said Sid, leaning back and looking pleased. "Now, before you leave here I want to give you a task, okay? Because that's the thing in bullshitdom—people say, 'Well, that's very good, we'll be back in touch' and so on. I mean, what is *that*? So we've both got to be working on this thing. We need to compile a Bible. You know what a Bible is? It's all the documentation we can possibly use. Give me letters, pictures, court orders, warrants, affidavits, everything you've got. Can you do that for me?"

"Sure," I said. "In fact, I've brought a lot of that stuff with me."

"Then let's Xerox what you've got," said Sid, leading me to an adjoining room. "And then get the fee to me, all right? I'm going to need the fee right away."

"I tell you what, Sid," I said expansively as we waited for the Xerox machine to warm up. "My trustee's right around the corner. I'll tell him to put it in the mail on Monday."

Sid looked startled. "In the mail?" he said. "What the hell is that? You know what the mail's like around here? Look, they got little hunchbacks on bikes in this city. Messengers. You call up your trustee, you have him send it over by messenger, okay?"

"Uh, all right," I said. "I'll have him send it over on Monday."

"Good, okay," said Sid, leaning toward me as I began to feed my stuff into the copier. "But look, Tom, I'd be a liar if I told you that I'm only going to cost you five thousand dollars. Because I'm actually going to cost you ten."

17

ABRAMSON

It's hard to explain my attitude toward Sid's fee. On the one hand my hackles rose because here he'd made a great show of laying out his terms ahead of time, and I was facing an additional three to five thousand dollars for Abramson's fee, and now Sid was already doubling his own fee to ten thousand.

There was a kind of supplication in Sid's eyes as we stared at each other, but it wasn't just the money he was asking for. It was proof of my trust in him. I could already see that there was something in Sid that said, "For God's sake, believe in me, because if you don't I'm just going to deflate, and then there won't be anything in this for either of us." I wondered if he expected me to haggle with him, if he'd lose all respect for me if I didn't. But I suddenly sensed that if I dickered with Sid, if I even suggested that he wasn't worth ten thousand dollars to me, he might collapse. I needed him puffed up, full of himself, ready for bear. It wasn't really his energy or even his creativity I needed. It was his audacity, his direct line to the heart of the problem.

Maybe Sid had merely succeeded in getting me to think the way he thought, but as I stood there gaping at him in the Xerox room, the proposition boiled down to this: I had the money; I didn't have the kids. Reversing that equation was worth ten thousand, fifteen thousand—everything I had. Simply believing in someone again after all those weeks was worth the candle.

"All right," I said, holding out my hand to him. "It's a deal."

Looking back on it now I realize that Hill's initial advice to me had been substantially the same as Sid's: get an Israeli lawyer and a detective and go get the kids. The difference was that where Kugler was ready to take charge, Hill would not approach my problem comprehensively. Hill had given me what he called jiffy service—he'd filed briefs, made motions, logged a few grudging phone calls. But wherever my problem involved questions that weren't covered by law, and only civil law at that, he'd thrown up his hands. As far as Hill was concerned, coordinating an "operation"—laying down all the lines, making the calls, checking everyone out, setting it all down beforehand—was just not "lawyer's business."

But Sid refused to let some arcane concept of a lawyer's function obscure my problem or deny its complexity, and he didn't regard civil procedures, whether Israeli or American, as not only appropriate to my circumstance but inexorable. He was the first person I'd dealt with who'd seen past the legalisms to the heart of my problem: I wanted my children home.

So ten thousand or no ten thousand, Susan and I floated out of Sid's office that noon.

A storm came blasting down the coast that Sunday, and Susan and I sat through it in the living room, reviewing all our notes and documents to pass along to Sid the next morning.

Gazing out the window that afternoon I caught sight of something bobbing around off the beach, and I went out in my slicker to investigate. It turned out to be an unmarked little wooden dinghy that had broken loose from its moorings somewhere up the coast.

I waded out and pulled it up onto the beach. The dinghy was pretty beat-up, with a big gash along its bow, so I hauled it to the boathouse, where Susan found me an hour later, trying to patch it up.

"What do you want with such a tiny boat?" she asked, ducking in from the rain.

"It's going to be a Christmas present for Ben and Sara," I heard myself reply. "We're going to get them back."

Susan smiled and embraced me and left me alone with the boat for the rest of the afternoon.

In the meantime Flynn had somehow persuaded the phone company in Colorado to give him an Israeli number that had turned up on Kitty's phone bill, which Ripkin, the liaison officer, traced to the same address Barbara had recorded: 445/3 Padkin Street.

On Wednesday the Israeli consulate called to report that the Ministry of Foreign Affairs in Jerusalem had confirmed Barbara's entry into Israel on Ben and Sara's birthday and had found there was no record of their having left. I relayed all this to Sid, who promised to include it in the Bible he was compiling for Abramson.

"It's going out by courier," he told me. "Oh, and by the way, Saul called back and said this Marcus character's last name is Fleischer."

"Fleischer!" I said. "Sid, that's great! How did he find out?"

"How do I know?" Sid said equably. "As far as I know the diamond business is just a bunch of guys with briefcases running around Antwerp. But I've given the name to Abramson's detective, and he's going to check it out."

"That's terrific," I said. "He's got to be the key to this thing."

"Maybe," said Sid. "Maybe not. I don't know about any keys."

On November 22nd I received a letter from Gerald Miller at the State Department confirming that Ben and Sara's names had been flagged in the computer. Enclosed was some literature about further assistance the State Department could provide.

Evidently there was something called the Office of Citizens Consular Services that handled everything from lost passports to transferring deceased American tourists back to the States. Their Near East and South Asia desk was run by a woman named Joan Billings, so I gave her a call and asked if she would request the American embassy in Tel Aviv to find out if Barbara had filed for Israeli citizenship or initiated any civil action in court.

"You know, Mr. Osborne," she said gently, "I have eleven cases on my desk right now exactly like yours. There isn't very much I can do to help you, but I'll put in a request at the embassy in Tel Aviv to keep an eye out for your kids."

"Can you find out if Barbara's applied for citizenship or maybe filed some kind of civil action in court?"

"I can try, Mr. Osborne," she said, "but you know most of these cases are handled by the parents themselves. If you can avoid the courts over there you should do it."

"What are you telling me, to kidnap my kids?"

"Well," she said, "you know I can't really advise that. Why don't you just give me the information, and I'll see what I can do?"

I had no expectations left for Ms. Billings to disappoint. My hopes lay elsewhere now, and on Friday morning, December 2nd, Susan and I returned to Sid's office to meet with Abramson.

Jacob Abramson arrived a little late, a trim, white-haired gentleman with thick dark eyebrows and deeply set, somewhat melancholy eyes. He greeted Susan by taking her hand and raising it almost to his lips.

"What a very great pleasure," he said, bowing slightly.

He completely changed gears for me, grabbing my hand and my elbow in both hands and giving my arm a vigorous shake. "Mr. Osborne," he said. "I'm so pleased to meet you."

Abramson's manner was courtly, almost continental, and as we all sat down I could see Sid pulling up his tie.

"Mr. Abramson," Sid said, "I want you to know how much we appreciate your taking an interest in this case. Did you get the material we sent?"

"Yes," Abramson replied. "Everything seems to me to be in order. There seem to me sufficient warrants and court orders and stipulations to provide us with a fall-back position. The law is on your side, Mr. Osborne, but there is no doubt in my mind that the way to handle this is as an operation."

"Operation" sent something of a chill down my back. "But if the law's on my side, why shouldn't we go through the courts?"

"Your right to the children would probably be recognized eventually," Abramson said, turning toward me. "But you must remember that the court wouldn't necessarily be bound by the terms of an American settlement because the children are in Israel, after all, and whether or not they finally recognize your former wife's conversion, which I very much doubt, she is their natural mother and she is probably seeking citizenship."

"Messy," said Sid.

"Very messy," Abramson agreed, setting his elbows on the arms of his chair and clasping his hands together. "If we could rely entirely on the courts, if we could keep control of the situation, then that would be fine. But the problem is that Israeli legal procedures are open to all kinds of shenanigans. Your wife could seek to have the jurisdiction switched around, could request delays to gather information, and even if in the end she got turned down, the delay could get us pinned down over there forever."

"And in the meantime?" Sid asked.

"And in the meantime," Abramson said with a nod, "the children would automatically be remanded to your former wife, and if her past performance is anything to go by, there wouldn't be anything to prevent her from making off with them again."

"And even if she didn't make off with them, Tom," Sid said, swiveling his chair toward me, "you can imagine what we'd be putting the children through."

"That's right," said Abramson.

"Everything would be up in the air," said Sid. "There'd be these lawyers jerking them around. There'd be all these stories floating around within their earshot, and it would be poison. They wouldn't know what to believe. And all for what? To reconfirm a custody agreement?"

I stared back for a moment at Abramson and Sid. It seemed strange to hear two lawyers advising against going to court, and I could feel my breathing tighten up as I began to contemplate what Abramson and Sid might mean by an "operation."

"But this 'operation' idea is going to be risky, too, isn't it?"

Abramson and Sid glanced at each other. "There's no question," said Abramson. "But only to the extent to which Barbara's put them at risk. Any way we handle this there is going to be risk, but there is current risk, real risk, in our not doing anything. What we need to devise is a means of getting the children out that minimizes the risks—the risk of physical harm, emotional harm, the risk of getting caught and winding up in court."

"Which means we have to think everything through ahead of time," said Sid.

"And be prepared to act quickly when the opportunity arises," Abramson said.

"But act how?" I wanted to know. "What do you propose?"

"First we must understand the premise," said Abramson, raising one finger. "You must recognize that your wife has taken the children to a besieged country. Israel's security system is the tightest in the world. We therefore can't do anything that might raise an alarm."

"Like?" asked Susan.

"Like go to the American embassy in Tel Aviv and apply for travel vouchers for the children."

"But that's the only way—" I began to say.

"I'm sorry," said Abramson sternly, "but you have to get separate passports for the children."

"But I've already tried that," I said. "It's a brick wall."

"There must be a way," Abramson said. "You can't just pick up the kids and then stand in line with them for travel vouchers. It could raise all kinds of alarm. The American embassy is absolutely the wrong place to touch base in an operation like this."

"Look," I said, "even if I tried to get passports they all know me in Boston. The FBI knows me, the U.S. Attorney. They're all in the same building. They've all been alerted to this thing."

Abramson shrugged. "Then go to another city," he said.

"But even that won't work," I said. "The kids' names are flagged in the State Department computer. Now if anyone applies for a passport for them this guy Miller is going to put the kibosh on it."

Sid and Abramson looked at each other. "Well, then," said Abramson with his eyebrows raised, "you're going to have to tell him to take their names out."

"But he'll wonder why. He'll ask a lot of questions."

Abramson's eyes seemed to freeze. "Call him," he said.

"Now?"

"Call him now."

I didn't realize it at the time, but it occurs to me that Abramson was probably testing me, seeing if I had the wit or the guts to follow through on the operation. I went off to an adjoining room and called Gerry Miller.

Gerry said he remembered me and asked if I'd had any word about the kids.

"Well, Gerry," I said, "that's why I'm calling. I'm calling to ask if you could take the kids' names off the computer."

"I could," Gerry said, "but do you mind if I ask you why you want me to do that?"

"Look," I said, trying to think fast, "everything's been resolved. But my wife's attorney is concerned that if anything happened to me in the future she wouldn't be able to get passports."

"Oh, I understand the situation," Gerry said brightly. "That wouldn't be a problem, Tom. I think we'd better just leave them on. Tom, I don't want to be downbeat about this, but sometimes you work things out, and they don't stay worked out, you know? So it'll be better to leave them on."

I turned my back to the door. "Gerry," I said, "I would really like you to take them off, and I'm kind of asking you to do this. I need the cooperation of my government in this, and I haven't gotten much so far, and this is something I'm asking you to do, and there's no reason for you not to do it."

"Ah," he said after a pause. "So you're about to take a trip?"

"Look," I said, "I don't want to answer that question, because I don't want to put you in an embarrassing position, and I don't want to put myself in an embarrassing position, and I don't want to screw everything up. I'm just asking you to take the names off."

There was another long pause, and Gerry said, "Well, Tom, send me a letter, and I'll see what I can do."

"Good," Sid said when I returned to his office. "I'm going to Washington tomorrow. Write a letter to Miller and I'll mail it there. Just to get this request on the record."

"If I get the passports," I said, "what next?"

"I've got a detective on the case," Abramson replied. "As a matter of fact he's got the address you gave me and the kids' pictures you sent, and he's starting today."

"Just so long as he doesn't alert Barbara," said Sid.

"That's been made clear to him," said Abramson. "He's very good, very discreet. He's going to start with the schools."

"So if he finds the kids—"

"*When* he finds the kids," Sid interjected. "Look, Tom, we're going to find them. I mean, figure it out. We've got the address from two sources. And even if they've moved, somebody's going to know where they went. Nobody can hide. Two red-headed American kids hiding in Israel? Forget it. We'll find them."

Abramson nodded to me. "Once he's found the kids he reports back to me. He should let me know within two weeks. I've told him not to do anything to alert Barbara."

"She's got to be expecting something," I said. "She must know I'm going to come after her."

"He'll be careful," Abramson said. "And as soon as I hear anything I'll call you. So be prepared to move fast. You've got to have your own passports ready and your visas and all the rest of it. I don't think there's anything to restrict your entry into Israel, but I'm going to check around and make sure."

"So we pick up the kids," I said. "Then what?"

"Then you get the hell out of Israel," said Sid, glancing at Abramson.

"But how?" asked Susan.

"I've been exploring that question," Abramson said. "I don't know about the airports. They're pretty tight. But so are the border crossings, and Barbara could raise an alarm before we could reach one of them."

Abramson shrugged. "I think our best bet might be a boat to Cyprus."

Susan and I looked at each other. "A boat to Cyprus?"

"Yes," said Abramson. "It's relatively safe. I've checked this out with my friends in the Ministry of Defense."

"Friends?" I asked.

"Yes," Sid broke in. "Didn't I tell you? Jake here was in the Israeli army for—how many years?"

Abramson shrugged. "My friends tell me the Palestinians aren't interfering with boat traffic for some reason. And security isn't as tight on boats heading to Cyprus."

"Terrific," I said.

"I'm not saying that's the plan, Mr. Osborne," Abramson said. "But it's a possibility, and at this stage we must contemplate all the possibilities. We will decide together when you come to Israel.

"But remember this," he said, reaching forward and touching my arm. "You will be in control of the situation. We will not do anything you cannot accept. We will not subject your children to unnecessary risks. I will not allow any foolishness."

I stared hard at Abramson for a few seconds, and he kept his hand on my arm. All I had left now was my intuition, and Susan's, and the hope that I would get my children back. There was something inherently trustworthy about Abramson; his eyes conveyed enormous empathy and respect, and his voice was even and reassuring. I decided there was no turning back. I would invest my trust in Jacob Abramson.

"All right," I said. "I'll come when you tell me."

18

PASSPORTS

I still didn't know if Miller had removed Ben and Sara from his computer, but Abramson insisted that I had to acquire new passports for them immediately.

For this I was going to need pictures of Ben and Sara, so Susan and I scrambled through every box in the house looking for something suitable. Sara had had one of those little portraits taken for school in Bourne, and we finally came upon some passport-sized copies in an envelope carefully hidden away in her room.

But the only pictures I had of Ben were snapshots. One of them was a head-on portrait of him standing in the yard with a soccer ball, squinting into the sun, so I cropped it down to his head and had a local film shop make passport-sized copies. The result was a grainy, marginal likeness, but it was the best we could find, and armed with their pictures and birth certificates, Susan and I flew down to Washington on Thursday, December 8th.

I kept rehearsing my lie to the passport office. It went something like this: my children were staying with my aunt in Boston, and she had just called to tell me that she had lost their passports, and I needed to replace them in order to take my children overseas for the holidays.

I'd tried it out on Sid, but he had put his hands over his ears. "Tom," he'd said, "I'm not advising you on that. It seems to me the passports are missing because the kids are missing, but I can't tell

165

you to break the law. All I can tell you is to call me if you get into trouble."

The passport office was in a big modern office tower in downtown Washington. The receptionist handed me the form for lost passports, and I sat down on a couch in the lobby and began to fill it out.

It asked a lot of questions: how were the passports lost? Were the police called? Did you take the following actions? So line by line I set down my lie in jittery script and balked a moment before signing a final statement swearing that the information I had given was true.

I carried the fraudulent application back to the receptionist. She was a large, bored black woman who looked at me a little dubiously as I slipped the form onto her desk.

Suddenly I found myself trying to explain myself. "Look, the thing is," I said, "you see I'm a professor visiting down here, and on Monday we're all supposed to go to France."

"That so?" the woman said with a shrug, flipping through the application.

"Yes," I said as Susan joined me. "Yes, you see, the kids are up in Boston with their aunt, and she just called me yesterday—was it yesterday?" I said, turning to Susan.

"I believe it was yesterday, yes," Susan said, nodding back.

"Yesterday," I said. "And she called me yesterday, and she said that the kids' passports had gone to France—that is," I said, with a shake of my head, "not gone to *France. Disappeared.* Disappeared, of course. So I told my aunt to send down their pictures and some birth certificates down by Federal Express, and she's done that and now they're here with the application. See?"

The woman was staring at me now.

"See?" I said, pointing to the application. "Are they going to be all right?"

"The children?" she asked.

"The pictures. Are the pictures going to be all right?"

The woman set my application down in an out basket. "I don't know," she said, writing a claim check for me. "That's for the people upstairs to figure out. You come in tomorrow afternoon."

As Susan escorted me out I kept looking over my shoulder at my application waiting like a time bomb in the out basket.

———

That night Susan and I stayed with my sister, who lived across from the Washington Zoo. I felt a chill in my stomach as I tried to sleep: a chill that wasn't to leave me for weeks, now that Abramson's wheels had been set in motion.

The next afternoon Susan walked with me from my sister's to the passport office, but outside the door I turned to her and told her not to come in with me.

"I may have some trouble in there," I said. "I don't want to get you involved."

"But I'm already involved," she said.

"No you're not," I said. "You're not on that form. If I get into trouble I'm going to need you on the outside, Susan."

Susan couldn't keep from rolling her eyes at me a little. "Oh come on, Tom," she said. "What do you mean, 'On the outside'? This isn't some movie."

"Look," I said. "I've just *lied*—"

"Shh," said Susan.

"I just lied to the *government*, Susan," I said, lowering my voice and glancing up and down the street.

"Well, the government's been lying to you."

"But if Miller's still got the kids tagged, they could arrest me. So you've got to wait for me back at my sister's. All right? Meet me back at my sister's at four."

Susan was still skeptical but went along with my paranoia and let me go in by myself.

The same lady managed the desk, and I nodded to her and handed her my claim check.

She slowly wet her fingers and sorted through a stack of manila envelopes on the desk in front of her.

"Not here," she said.

"You said they were going to be ready this afternoon."

"Well," she said, handing me back the claim check. "Afternoon isn't over yet. Wait over there, and I'll let you know."

I tried to be casual as I sank into an engulfing chair in the large, dim lobby. The afternoon dragged on. A family of newly naturalized Pakistanis came and proudly claimed their passports, the children giggling at their pictures as they departed. A dapper man in pinstripes hurried in and collected his, and then an elderly woman in sneakers.

It got to be three o'clock and then four o'clock, and by now I was convinced that Miller hadn't removed the flags, and all hell was about to break loose. Susan ventured in around four-thirty, but I waved her away from my perch in the lobby, and she continued around the revolving doors and stumbled back out onto K Street.

The woman at the desk and I had been exchanging looks off and on for almost three hours, and now I finally rose and asked her why there was a delay.

"I don't know. Everything's going to be all right," she said. "They'll be down. And if they don't come down they'll be down on Monday morning."

"Monday will be too late," I told her. "I'm going to Italy on Sunday."

"You're going to France," she said blandly.

"France," I said, "*then* Italy."

"Uh-huh," she said, resuming her work.

"Look," I said. "I've got to get out of here. Where's your supervisor? Let me talk to your supervisor."

The woman shrugged and picked up the phone. "Mr. Haughwat," she said. "Man wants to see you."

A pale, harried young man with a pen holster in his shirt pocket emerged from a neighboring door. "What is it, Rita?"

"Mr. Hyatt," I said.

"Haughwat," he said sharply.

"Mr. Haughwat," I said, "I'm Tom Osborne. I've been waiting three hours for my children's passports."

"Osborne, Osborne," he said. "Oh yeah," he said, tugging at his glasses. "You've got a problem."

I swallowed. "What problem?"

Haughwat peered at me a moment longer. "I don't know," he said, retreating back through his door. "They're working on it upstairs."

"Well, then let me talk to the person upstairs," I called after him as his door swung closed. "Who's in charge here?"

The door opened again slightly, and Haughwat poked his head around. "The man who's in charge of this building," he said peevishly, "is the man who's working on this problem, Mr. Osborne, and *I* for one am not going to disturb him."

Oh Christ, I thought as I retreated back into the lobby. *They've found me out.*

Now people were beginning to go home, and the guard was standing by the door, jingling his keys and wishing his fellow employees nice weekends. The receptionist's phone kept ringing, and she had several hushed conversations during which she seemed to glance at me from time to time. I considered leaving, but I seemed to be immobilized, sitting in my lobby chair and trying to work up some alternative rationale for the application.

The guard and I exchanged a couple of looks, and I was convinced that he and the receptionist had instructions to string me along until they could get security down to handcuff me. The receptionist was standing now and sticking things into her purse.

"What's going on up there?" I called over to her in a parched voice.

"I'm sorry, sir," she said, reaching for her coat. "You'll just have to wait."

I was becoming a little unhinged by now, and I suddenly got to my feet and slapped my forehead. "Wait a minute," I said. "*I* know what the problem is. These kids have got their names tagged in the *computer.* That's it, isn't it?"

The woman set down her coat and stared at me a moment. "Well," she said uncertainly, "as a matter of fact—"

"Oh," I said, "I can *explain* that."

"But why didn't you mention it earlier?" she said, reaching for the phone. "You could have saved us a lot of trouble."

"I—I just didn't think of it."

"Mr. Osborne says he knows the names are tagged," she said.

She listened a while, and then she slowly hung up and said, "All right, Mr. Osborne. It's going to be all right."

And at that moment Haughwat reemerged and grudgingly handed me Ben and Sara's passports.

Sid was delighted by my success at the passport office, and he immediately got on the horn to Abramson in Tel Aviv. Abramson congratulated me on my audacity, but had to report that he had had no word as yet from his detective. It was still early, he assured us, but usually the detective checked in daily, and Abramson hadn't heard from him for four days.

All this time I had remained in school as a kind of evasive action. I studied with some considerable ferocity and did well on my finals that next week. But I dreaded completing the semester. What was I going to do during my holidays with nothing to divert me from the hole in my life?

On the 14th of December, I received a letter from Miller, dated the previous day, reporting that he had removed Ben and Sara from the computer and warning me that he would now no longer be able to deny them passports. In the same day's mail was a letter from Joan Billings at the State Department reporting that the American embassy had learned from the Israeli Ministry of the Interior that there was no record of Barbara's having applied for citizenship.

As soon as my semester was over, everything seemed to grind to a halt. I called Sid every day, but he'd run out of news. Either he wouldn't have heard anything from Abramson or Abramson wouldn't have heard anything from his detective. Either way, nothing was happening.

"Just part of the process, Tom," Sid told me. "In every one of these things you're going to hit some dry patches. Just try to keep the faith."

But a week had gone by since I'd seen Abramson, and then another, and my old despair began to seep in again. That second week became like a microcosm of the preceding months of futility and frustration, only now there was nothing to do: no calls to make, no leads to follow, not even a class to attend. There was nothing to do but wait.

On the night of December 15th, I downed half a jug of cheap French wine. It had been almost three months since I'd seen the kids and now the detective's failure to find them had revived my worst imaginings. I was too exhausted to stave off my dread any longer. I couldn't believe in Sid or Abramson or anyone else. I told Susan that Sid and Abramson were a couple of shysters milking me dry, taking me for another goddamn ride. They weren't going to find my children. It was all smoke and mirrors. The children weren't even in Israel. By now they could have been anywhere.

"Goddamn it, Susan," I said, pacing around the living room, "if we're going to find the kids we're going to have to do it ourselves.

That's the goddamn lesson in all this. We've got to do it ourselves. I don't care about these bastard lawyers. We're going to Israel."

Susan was sober, but she didn't argue, because what I was proposing was actually a distillation of everything our experience had taught us. We couldn't depend on anybody. Nobody else gave a damn whether I ever saw my children again.

As soon as I picked up the phone and called TWA, I felt a surge of power, as if I were regaining a grip on my own destiny. I made reservations for the following Tuesday, December 20th, and it made me feel terrific. I was doing something again.

Then I realized it was afternoon in Israel and decided I would call Abramson and tell him that I was coming whether he liked it or not. I was disappointed in him, but I was feeling my oats again, too, and I relished the prospect of telling him that he was an asshole for not finding my kids.

So I called Abramson.

"Look," I said, "this is Tom Osborne in Alden, and I'm calling to tell you—"

Abramson cleared his throat. "Mr. Osborne," he said. "Isn't it three in the morning back there? I was going to call you."

"Well," I said, "you don't have to call me because I called you."

But Abramson cut me off again. "But I've got news, Mr. Osborne," he said. "Listen to me. The detective—he just came in tonight.

"Mr. Osborne, he's talked to Sara. He's found your kids."

I nearly dropped the phone. "Thank God," I said. "Is he sure? Is he sure it's Sara?"

"Absolutely. He's got the picture. She told him she's got a brother named Ben."

It was the happiest moment of my life, and for the longest while I couldn't speak.

"Mr. Osborne? Are you there?"

By now Susan was embracing me, and tears were rolling down my cheeks.

"Oh God, Mr. Abramson," I said. "I was just calling you to tell you we're coming on Tuesday."

"Well, you better push it up to Monday," said Abramson. "You've got some children to bring home."

19

BEST-LAID PLANS

As Abramson later pieced it together for me, the detective had evidently gone to Hadera six days before and approached the headmaster of the local school, asking matter-of-factly if Ben and Sara were enrolled.

Ordinarily this was the most reliable means of determining the whereabouts of abducted children: school officials were usually cooperative, and the rolls were public record.

But this time the detective's inquiries had sounded an alarm. "Why do you want to know about our children?" the headmaster demanded to know. "Who are you to be asking these questions? You get out or we are calling the authorities."

So the detective had retreated for a few of days, hoping the school would calm down again. He then contrived one morning to stall his car near the playground, hoping to catch a glimpse of Ben and Sara. As he fumbled busily in the vicinity of his muffler, a class of children came racing out for recess, and among them he thought he recognized a thin, red-headed girl who stood somewhat apart from the other children as they fanned out across the playground.

The detective called over to her in English and told her that he bet he could guess her name. The girl approached him cautiously and said she bet he couldn't either, and he told her that her name was Sara and that she had a brother named Ben.

Sara beamed at him and was asking him to tell her how he'd

guessed, when suddenly a car screeched up to the curb, and two large policemen grabbed the detective and drove him away.

He was immediately taken to a police station, where he was rushed into an interrogation room and surrounded by angry cops demanding to know who he was and what he was after.

"Look," he said, "what's wrong with you people? What have I done?"

"That's exactly what we're going to find out," one of the cops said. "Who are you? What were you doing talking to that child?"

The detective considered manufacturing a cover story but thought better of it as the cops glowered at him. "I'm a detective," he said. "I am an ex-cop. I'm on a job, trying to find a couple of American kids who are living here."

The police examined the detective's personal papers and made a few calls, and after a couple of hours they released him, warning him not to go near the school again.

"But what was this all about?" he asked, as they ushered him outside.

"We're all on edge," one of the cops told him. "The whole town's in mourning. A little girl was murdered here last Tuesday."

All I could take in at first was that my children were alive. Just a few weeks before I hadn't been able to believe in anything; now I seemed to believe in everything again: Christmas, family, the future.

On the 16th, I put a final coat of paint on the little dinghy in the boathouse, and Susan fashioned a Christmas tree out of a cluster of branches she'd sprayed silver. We shopped for Ben and Sara's gifts in Hammond and rewrapped the birthday presents that had been gathering dust in the coat closet. Up to then I'd been unable to bear the sound of Christmas carols, but now I tuned them in and hummed along like a redeemed Scrooge.

That weekend we drove into Boston to deliver our presents to Aunt Jane. As we rang the doorbell I thought of Uncle Henry calling after me from his terrace that we would all be singing carols together by Christmas. Aunt Jane asked if we planned to join the rest of the family at her home on Christmas Day. Susan and I looked at each other and told her we were going to be taking a trip.

"Bring them back safely," she said after a searching pause. "Look," she said, pointing to the pile of gifts under her tree. "I've bought presents for them, too."

On Monday, December 19th, the car behaved strangely on the way to the airport, balking and chittering as I pulled into long-term parking. We were traveling light, but we'd packed some of the kids' clothes in among our own.

My mood was still jubilant. When I spotted a child's microscope in the duty-free shop I bought it for Ben and Sara. I tried to tuck it into my carry-on bag but it wouldn't fit, and I had to carry it under my arm as Susan looked on indulgently.

Our flight was to Tel Aviv with a few hours' stopover in Paris. It wasn't until we took our seats on the 747 that evening that I began to wonder if, as Abramson had put it, I had the stomach for an "operation." As we pulled up into the gloom over the Atlantic the enormity of what we were undertaking began to pound away at me. I felt as though I were moving inexorably toward some unimaginable catastrophe.

Susan tried to hold me together, but by the time we reached Paris she was ready for a break. She toured the duty-free shops at Orly airport as I sat gloomily in the lounge.

A bald Israeli in army fatigues and combat boots sat across from me with a huge, travel-stickered suitcase over which he'd painted "God helps those who help themselves" in sloppy, looping strokes. He kept nodding and smiling at me, and as I sat brooding he seemed to mutate into a monster of my own paranoia. What if he was one of Marcus's boys? What if Marcus had connections to Israeli intelligence? What if Barbara already knew I was on my way? What in hell was I flying into?

On the night of December 20th we landed in Tel Aviv and Abramson met us at the gate and drove us around his city. He obviously saw the anxiety in our eyes and did his best to divert us, pointing out the sights along the route to the hotel. He treated us like tourists, or perhaps more like children of his who had come to visit, never mentioning the operation, pointing out various local sights with obvious pride.

I don't know what I'd been expecting of Tel Aviv—gun emplacements perhaps, checkpoints, Arabs glaring at us from street corners: certainly not the bustling, rather bland seaside metropolis in which we suddenly found ourselves. We checked into an airy room with sea views Abramson had reserved for us, and then he took us down the street to a little cafe where families sat outside consuming fruit juice and pastries.

It was cool that evening, but I sweltered in my stateside sweater and jacket as Abramson walked us back to the hotel and arranged for us to meet him at his office the following afternoon. In the meantime he insisted that we rest and explore Tel Aviv and keep our minds off the operation.

Abramson seemed relaxed himself, even more relaxed than he'd been back in Sid's office. As Susan and I settled in I remember standing by the open window and breathing in the salt air: the same air, it occurred to me, that my children were breathing somewhere out in the dark.

Jet lag had us up by five-thirty the next morning, and we breakfasted in our room on herring, fruit, and yogurt. We tried to kill the morning by taking a bus tour that took us through old Jaffa and along the waterfront. I wondered if we would soon be embarking with the kids from the ramshackle piers on a voyage to Cyprus, and I imagined us slipping off in a flashlit rowboat as searchlights swept the water.

The tour took us to the top of Sholom Tower, the tallest building in Israel, with its shimmering views of the stucco city and the Mediterranean stretching out into the distance. No amount of sightseeing could assuage my yearning to lay eyes on Ben and Sara, but as we descended from the top of Sholom Tower we ran into a great tide of schoolchildren. Suddenly afraid Ben and Sara might be among them and inadvertently give us away to Barbara, I ducked into a doorway until the schoolchildren passed.

That afternoon we took a taxi to Abramson's office, a whitewashed room with a sea view in a residential section of Tel Aviv. Abramson greeted us in slacks and a sport shirt and introduced us to the detective who'd found Sara: an edgy, disheveled young man named Mordecai Alterman.

The first thing I wanted from Alterman was more details about Sara. How was she? Was she well? Was her voice clear? Did she seem happy?

"She seemed . . . fine," he said deliberately, glancing uneasily at Abramson.

"You'll soon see for yourself," Abramson said, showing us to some chairs encircling a cluttered coffee table.

Abramson slapped his knees and looked around at us. "Well?" he said finally. "Anyone got any ideas?"

Susan and I looked at each other. I could feel the chill reasserting itself in the pit of my stomach.

"I thought you'd thought this through," I said. "I thought everything had been set up already."

"Well," said Abramson, "we still need to figure out how to get you out of the country."

"But you said Cyprus—"

"No," he said. "Mordecai here says there's been a lot of activity along the coast and security's been stepped up."

"Yes," said Alterman. "They've increased their patrols. They caught some more Palestinians sneaking in on a raft."

"So we'll fly?" I asked.

"You can't fly out," said Abramson.

"Why not?" asked Susan.

"Because airport customs is extremely efficient. If Barbara sounds an alarm, they'll be the first to hear it."

"And," said Alterman, "all forms of public transportation are out. The buses are constantly checked, there are too many police working in the taxi companies, and all the cabs have radios. It's too risky."

"Yes," said Abramson. "Much too risky."

"Then where does that leave us?" I wanted to know. "What other way *is* there?"

"By car?" Abramson asked, turning toward Alterman.

"Yes, by car."

"But by car to where? To Jordan? Syria? To *Lebanon*, for God's sake?"

The detective shook his head. "To Egypt," he said.

"Egypt?" I said. "Wait a minute. Isn't Israel technically at war with Egypt?"

"Not any longer," said Abramson patiently. "Not since Camp David."

"But isn't it dangerous?"

Abramson shrugged. "Let's reason this out together. We can't fly, we can't sail. We must get you out by land. Jordan is out. Syria is out. Lebanon, of course, is out of the question. But the traffic's fairly open between Egypt and Israel. Tourists have begun to go back and forth along the Gaza Strip."

"But where would we cross?" Susan asked.

"Rafah," said Alterman, unfolding a map on the coffee table. "It's a new crossing set up by the Camp David agreement. It's not as well established. It would take a long time for an alarm to reach it."

"Would we go straight along the coast?" Abramson asked as we all leaned over the map. Israel looked to me for a moment as though its neighbors were pushing it into the sea. "That would be the shortest route."

"Shortest," said Alterman, "but not necessarily the safest."

"So what do you suggest?" I said, scanning inland from the coast.

"Here," said Alterman, running his hand along the Jordanian border.

"East?" said Abramson, rubbing his chin. "Yes, I see what you mean."

I looked up at the two of them as they nodded at each other. "Wait a minute," I said. "That's the goddamn West Bank."

"The disjuncture," Abramson said to Alterman, ignoring me.

"Yes," said Alterman.

I tapped my knuckles on the map. "What are you talking about?"

Alterman and Abramson looked at me. "This is our thinking," Abramson said. "Hadera is under civil jurisdiction. The West Bank is under the military. If Barbara sounds an alarm with the police, there's no telling how swiftly it'll travel through the civil jurisdiction. But crossing into a military jurisdiction will slow down the alarm and give us time to reach the border."

"And Mr. Abramson here has more influence with the military," said Alterman. "He can get us through the checkpoints."

Abramson shrugged. "Perhaps," he said softly.

"But the West Bank—" Susan said.

"—has its hazards, no question," said Abramson.

"The Palestinians are always throwing stones at cars. They toss them over the walls of the orchards," Alterman volunteered. "And if a car breaks down there's a fair chance we might get attacked. Maybe I should take a gun along."

Abramson glowered at Alterman and stood at the window for a moment.

"You don't have a permit," he said.

"But if we did get stopped we could defend ourselves," said Alterman.

"And if we did get stopped by the army, which is far more likely, I would be disbarred, and you would be arrested."

"It's worth the risk, isn't it?"

"No," said Abramson grimly, sitting down again. "It isn't worth the risk. No gun."

Alterman looked crestfallen. I didn't know if I was relieved by this decision or alarmed. Then again, I couldn't have been more alarmed than I was already. Palestinians. Stones. Patrols. Guns. The whole thing seemed to be spinning out of control.

"Now then," said Abramson, "I've been giving the timing some thought. I suggest Friday. The courts here close on Friday afternoon, Mr. Osborne, and that's good, because that will make it that much more difficult for Barbara's lawyer to get a judge to sign a warrant."

"So we should go Friday afternoon?" I asked.

"No," said Abramson. "The pickup's going to have to be Friday morning, when the children are on their way to school. Alterman knows their routine," Abramson said, giving Alterman a conciliatory nod.

"Yes," said Alterman. "They leave their apartment at seven-thirty and walk four blocks to school, although they are often late."

That figures, I thought. "So why not pick them up on their way back from school?" I asked.

"Because the border crossing at Rafah closes at noon," said Abramson. "And it takes four hours to get there."

Susan and I stared at each other. Somehow Abramson's reasoning was penetrating my fear and sinking into my consciousness. But it all seemed so outlandish. Susan was a potter from Minnesota. I was an associate professor of history. What was I doing in Tel Aviv, Israel, discussing such things?

"We'll need two cars," said Alterman. "One to take us to Hadera, and another for the drive to Rafah."

"Yes," said Abramson. "I've thought of that. We can use yours as far as Hadera, and then take mine to Rafah."

"Yours?" asked the detective. "You mean the Peugeot?"

"Yes, the Peugeot," said Abramson.

"But Mr. Abramson, it's got a couple hundred thousand miles on it."

"Yes," said Abramson. "But I am having it rebuilt. By Friday it'll be as good as new."

Alterman shrugged dubiously.

"So," said Abramson, "are we forgetting anything?"

Susan and I swallowed hard. "What about Hadera?" I said.

"What about it?"

"That child's murder. Isn't everyone going to be watching the kids like hawks?"

Immediately I felt outraged that Barbara had managed to cast me now as a conspirator in a foreign land, plotting a route around the grieving, vigilant mothers and fathers of Hadera.

"Yes," Abramson allowed sadly. "It isn't helpful."

"All it means," said Alterman, puffing out his chest a little, "is that we must be quick about it. In, out. No complications."

Abramson looked at Alterman disapprovingly. "All it means," he said slowly, "is that we must be careful, Mordecai. We must do nothing to raise an alarm." Abramson turned to me. "But we must get your children out of there."

Alterman squirmed uncomfortably and shrugged.

"It's going to work," Abramson said, nodding to us. "But first you must do some things at your end. Tell the hotel you will be going out for an expedition to Jerusalem Friday morning and won't be back until late evening. Pay in advance for another night at the hotel, and in the morning leave all your luggage in your room. This way the staff will think you're coming back, and that will reassure Barbara's lawyer if he comes sniffing around the hotel. All right? Is that clear?"

"Yes," I said, grabbing a legal pad off the coffee table and jotting down a note.

"And you will need to write a note," he said. "A note to Barbara."

"Saying what?"

Abramson thought for a while. "It must reassure her, but it must be firm."

"I'll tell her I've taken the children to Jerusalem for a—a Christmas outing," I said, warming to the plan at last. "I'll tell her that I have a right to do that."

"Good," said Alterman.

"And I'll tell her that I'll bring the children back in the evening, but in the meantime I'm going to need their passports."

"Passports?" said Abramson.

"Yes," I said. "I'll tell her that I haven't come to take the kids back, but my lawyer wants to arrange to pick up the passports because he's advising me that it would be safer to have them along while we're touring Israel."

"But she will never give Mr. Abramson the passports," said Alterman.

"That's just it," said Abramson, winking at me. "She'll keep the passports and think she's in control of the situation. If she thinks we won't be able to leave the country without the passports, she might not blow the whistle on us right away."

"Right," I said, nodding back at him.

"Ah," said Alterman. "That's good. And if she has any questions you can tell her to call Mr. Abramson at home."

"Yes," said Abramson. He thought a moment. "But I won't be home. I'll have my sister tell her to call me at my office, and then I'll have my secretary tell her I'm out of the office, and so on. That should buy us some time.

"So," Abramson said, turning back to Susan and me, "we drive to Hadera, pick up the kids, drop off the letter, switch cars, drive down the West Bank, cross at Rafah into Egypt. Are we agreed?"

I balked a moment and stared at Susan. It occurred to me that none of the measures countries took ostensibly to protect children had been effective in protecting my children from abduction, but now those same measures were working against us: the computer tags, the passport restrictions, and now the frightened vigilance of Hadera. What Abramson was proposing was that I now become an abductor myself.

But it seemed to me that the dangers we faced were dangers the children had been facing for three months, compounded by Barbara's negligence and impulsiveness. I could barely weigh one risk against another anymore, but it seemed to me that the only safety for my children lay with me, at home, whatever it was going to take to get them there.

"Tom?" Susan said, touching my arm.

"Agreed," I said, as Abramson held out his hand.

20

VISAS

Abramson invited us to have dinner with his sister and him Thursday night at his apartment in Jaffa and sent us back to the hotel in a taxi. I kept running through the plan that night, wondering what we'd forgotten. There didn't seem to be any fall-back position if we got caught. I would be within my rights as a custodial father with valid passports for the kids, but what if the Israelis didn't see it that way? What if they somehow regarded me as an outlaw stealing one of their people's children?

Susan and I ate at the hotel and fretted over the letter to Barbara. I tried to keep it matter-of-fact, but my anger kept intruding, and it took several drafts before I could sound the right note. She had to disbelieve the reason I gave for requesting the kids' passports, and yet she had to believe the rest of it: that for the time being at least, I was merely taking the kids around for a little Christmas excursion. I told her that there was a felony warrant out for her arrest, a copy of which I enclosed. I told her I didn't want to make her life any more difficult than it already was, but if she did anything to interfere with my visit with the kids I would send a copy of the warrant to the Israeli police.

Abramson called around ten that night to tell us that he'd just re-membered that Israelis needed to obtain visas in order to get into Egypt. He wasn't sure if that applied to Americans as well, but he advised us to check at the Egyptian embassy in the morning to find out.

Having never been to the Middle East, I had imagined that we would go to the Egyptian embassy and a receptionist would usher me in and give us the visas. But when the cabby dropped us off at ten o'clock on Thursday morning, we found a block-long line leading up to a little ramshackle booth set against the side of the embassy.

I somehow assumed that the line wasn't for us, walked directly into the embassy, and found the receptionist I had envisioned: a crisp, westernized woman filing her nails.

"We're here to obtain visas," I said.

"You must wait outside," she said sternly, lowering her nail file.

"I just thought—" I said, drawing out our passports from my jacket with an ingratiating smile.

"Go outside," she said. "You must wait like all the others."

So Susan and I limped outside and took our places at the end of the line. It moved like molasses, and ahead of us we could see the shutters to the visa booth open and close as a grimly phlegmatic clerk referred various applications to his superiors.

A small boy in khaki pants spotted us as we slowly shuffled forward. "Pictures, sir," he said, tugging at my sleeve. "You must have pictures. No visa without pictures."

Susan and I couldn't figure out if he was a huckster or not, but we couldn't take any chances. We had some copies of the kids' pictures but none of ourselves, so we figured that since we were still pretty far down the line, we'd better duck over and have our pictures taken.

So we wound up sitting for mug shots in a dusty little studio across the road and wasted another hour waiting for them to be developed before returning to the line.

It didn't seem to have moved at all in the meantime: there were at least an additional twenty people ahead of us now. The booth was closed for almost half an hour, and I asked the Israeli in front of me when it was scheduled to open again.

He was a small, wry man in wire-rim spectacles. "When does it open? When does it close? Who can say?" he said. "They open and close it when they feel like it. I've been here ten times, and still I don't have a visa. Maybe I'll never get a visa. Who can say?"

184 · A Cry of Absence

"But I can't wait until tomorrow. I've got to get them before tomorrow. We're leaving tomorrow."

"Today, tomorrow, the next day," the small man said with a shrug.

In a few minutes the booth opened again, but the line moved almost imperceptibly. It got to be eleven o'clock, then noon, and then inexplicably the line began really to move, as if someone in the booth had suddenly woken up. Soon we were fifth in line, fourth, and then third and then second. I got the passports and the pictures out and stepped forward as the small man walked away satisfied, and suddenly the phlegmatic Egyptian pulled the shutters closed.

"Wait a minute," I shouted, and I knocked on the shutters with my fist.

"We are closed," came a voice from within. "You must come back Monday."

"Monday?" I said. "What do you mean, *Monday?*"

The bespectacled man turned around. "Tomorrow's a Moslem holiday. Saturday's a Jewish holiday. Sunday's a Christian holiday," he said with a sympathetic smile. "Welcome to the Holy Land."

I turned around and banged on the shutter again. "We've been here all morning. You can't just close the door in my face. You can't treat people this way."

I couldn't believe it. It seemed to sum up my entire experience with officialdom, and I wasn't going to put up with it anymore. By now several of the people behind me were cheering me on. I strode to the front of the embassy and began to rant and rave in front of the guard.

He seemed bored with my outburst and poked at his gums with a toothpick as I shouted at him. "You should be ashamed for treating people like this," I told him. "Your country should be ashamed. I demand to see the ambassador."

This gave my audience a big laugh, of course, because there hadn't been an Egyptian ambassador to Israel in six months. The guard obviously regarded me as an irritant and dealing with irritants was part of his job, part of his training. He gave me a lot of shrugs and flashed the crowd a few grins. I was obviously getting nowhere.

A very smooth Egyptian diplomat emerged from the embassy and climbed into a chauffeured Mercedes. As I was waving my arms around he instructed his driver to wait a minute and watched me through his tinted window.

So I started my speech over again, and finally the diplomat climbed out and walked over to me. "All right, all right," he said, addressing the guard. "What is the problem?"

The guard said something in Arabic, and now I started in on the diplomat: I'd waited in the goddamn line for three hours, it was a disgrace to the Egyptian people, they ought to be ashamed of themselves.

The diplomat heard me out for a minute and finally held out his hand. "Give me your passports," he said. "I will get you your visas. Come back at two o'clock."

"I need visas for Susan and me and my children," I said.

"No, no, no," he said, handing the children's passports back. "Only you and your wife. The children don't need visas."

I didn't like giving up our passports to this fellow, and I walked away feeling suddenly like a hostage to the Egyptian embassy. What if he were simply getting rid of me and intended to sit on our passports until Monday?

Susan and I limped off for lunch and returned to the embassy around one-thirty to get a jump on the line, only to find the same thing all over again: the line went around the block, and the booth was closed. It got to be two o'clock, two-thirty, and I lost my temper again.

"Susan," I said. "Wait here. I'm going around front."

I began to march on the guard again when the booth shutters suddenly swung open. People broke from the line and pressed forward like scavengers as a young man began to call out the numbers of our passports. After four hours in the midday sun, Susan and I finally had our Egyptian visas.

We tried to nap for the rest of the afternoon and then dressed for dinner at Abramson's. He lived on the top floor of a stucco apartment building a few blocks from his offic. He greeted us as we stepped out of our cab, shouting down to us from his balcony.

Abramson was a widower and lived with his sister, a very bright and energetic woman in her eighties who took a great shine to Susan and gave her a tour of the apartment as Abramson and I sat out on a little terrace overlooking the water. The breeze off the Mediterranean was warm and soothing, and sitting with Jake and taking deep draughts of a gin and tonic, I had to struggle to remember that the operation was only twelve hours away.

Abramson's sister let slip a few things about her brother: how he'd escaped from the Warsaw ghetto as a teenager and fought in the Polish resistance against the Nazis, how he'd remained in Poland and become a lawyer in order to assist Jews trying to emigrate, how he'd then fought in the Polish uprising against the Russians before finally escaping to Israel in 1957.

I warmed to Abramson as we dined on his sister's brisket and potato pancakes, and when this portrait emerged of Abramson as a principled man of action, I began to regain my confidence in the operation. Maybe he knew his business after all.

But then, as he drove us back to the hotel in his rebuilt Peugeot, he seemed to lose heart. I showed him the letter to Barbara, which he approved, but then he began to tell Susan how much he hated the whole operation.

"Why do people do this sort of thing?" he asked her vaguely. "Why does this sort of thing have to happen?"

I could see he was apprehensive. And if Jacob Abramson, former resistance leader and all-around mensch was anxious, how were Susan and I supposed to feel?

When we reached the hotel we went to the desk clerk as arranged. We told him we would be leaving early in the morning for Jerusalem, and wanted to pay for the next night's lodging in advance.

"Oh no, sir," he said. "We will keep your room. That won't be necessary."

"You don't understand," I said with a sinking feeling, for I'd somehow convinced myself that this was a crucial part of our deception, or in any case a small rehearsal. "We want to pay for the room ahead of time."

"No sir," he said graciously, "that really won't be necessary. We trust our guests to pay at the close of their visits."

"But I insist," I said, sliding my American Express card forward on the counter.

"No, no, Mr. Osborne. Really," he said, shaking his head and pushing the card back toward me. "It's against hotel policy."

I finally sighed and gave up. Susan at least managed to order box lunches for all of us, which the room clerk assured her would be ready by six. But it didn't seem to me a good sign that I couldn't pull off even the first ploy we'd been assigned.

I slept badly, of course. It seemed to me that if I couldn't even arrange to prepay the hotel, then there were bound to be more holes in the game plan that we couldn't possibly foresee: regulations at the checkpoints, missing documents, problems with the car. Overriding everything was the fact that we had given ourselves only four and half hours to get out of a town in which a child had been murdered and to drive down militarized back-country roads along most of the length of the most besieged nation on the face of the earth.

By midnight I'd lost every shred of confidence I had in the scheme. I told Susan it was just too dangerous. We were going to foul it up. We should have planned to take our chances at the airport. Not even my most paranoid fantasies could measure up to the hazards of this goddamn harebrained scheme.

Susan was apprehensive too, but however the question was going to be resolved, it seemed to her that it was bound to go in my favor.

"Go to sleep, Tom," she said. "It's going to work. These men know their business. All we can do now is get some sleep."

I tried to banish my fears with thoughts of Ben and Sara back in my arms, but what I saw as I finally dozed off in the predawn light was the mysterious Marcus Fleischer and his minions, lying in wait on the road to my children.

21

NO PLACE FOR CHILDREN

Susan and I rose at dawn on the morning of Friday, December 23rd, and went downstairs for breakfast, leaving everything behind in our room but an overnight bag with a few toiletries, a couple of sweaters, and the little microscope.

"Well," I told the bleary bellboy as he delivered a stack of box lunches, "we're off to Jerusalem for the day."

"Very good, sir," he said.

"Yes," I said, passing by the morning room clerk on the way out of the lobby, "off we go for our day in Jerusalem."

"Have a nice trip, sir," the room clerk said with a wave.

"Just for the day," I called out, stepping backwards past his desk. "We'll be back this evening," I was still saying as the revolving door cast me out onto the sidewalk.

Abramson was waiting for us in his station wagon, which idled noisily as the doorman stood by.

"See you this evening," I told the doorman as I climbed into the car and handed him a crumpled bill.

"Certainly, sir," he said, closing the door behind us.

Abramson paused and turned around to look at us. "Are you all right?" he said after giving me a searching look.

"Yes," I said, glancing over at Susan. "Yes, we're all set, aren't we, Susan?"

Abramson stared at me a moment longer and sighed. "All right then," he said, pulling out of the hotel drive.

He drove us through the hazy, sleeping city. We passed a couple of army jeeps, a milk truck, a couple of young Hassidim on bicycles pedaling off to worship, but otherwise the streets were as empty as my stomach.

"Mordecai will meet us in his car outside Hadera," Abramson said. "We're going to leave you with this car, Susan, and then Mordecai and Tom and myself will take his Fiat into town to pick up the children."

"Is that safe?" I said. "I mean, leaving Susan alone with the car?"

"Certainly," said Abramson with a little smile. "She won't steal it."

"I'll be all right," Susan said, though when she touched my arm her hand was cold and damp.

We drove through the northern outskirts of Tel Aviv and thirty miles along the coastal highway, through towns with names like Herzliya, Netanya, and Kfar Vitkin. Staring out at the arid empty spaces interspersed with urgent patches of greenery and sprinklers pulsing in the morning light, I tried to concentrate on Ben and Sara. What had their life been like these three months without me? Had they made friends in school? Had they missed me? What had Barbara told them about me? How had she explained their never having heard from me? Did they know about Uncle Henry's death?

We met Alterman at a little turnaround outside Hadera and switched cars, leaving Susan with the bag and the lunches in Abramson's old Peugeot.

"I'll see you soon," I said, giving her a quick embrace and climbing into the front seat. I meant to tell her that I loved her, that I could never have come this close to my children without her, but there was no time, and all I could do was wave back at her as Alterman drove us on into Hadera.

It was seven o'clock by the time we turned down Padkin Street and pulled up across from a pleasant little row of apartment buildings.

"They live there," Alterman said, pointing up at the third floor of 445, the central building: a pale pink stucco structure with wrought-iron balconies. I suppose I had been fantasizing them living in some tenement somewhere, certainly not on an upper-class street lined with palm trees.

We waited a long while that seemed longer because Alterman insisted on parking directly across the street from Barbara's apartment.

"Aren't we too close?" I asked Abramson. "What if Barbara comes out and sees us?"

"Don't worry about it," said Alterman. "She never gets up this early. She never gets out until ten."

"I don't know," said Abramson. "Why take a chance? Let's back it up a little in case she comes out."

"I'm for that," I said.

"Forget it," said Alterman, crossing his arms. "I know their routine. She won't see us."

"Mordecai," said Abramson, grabbing his shoulder from the back seat. "Back it up."

Alterman shook his head and lapsed into Hebrew and suddenly I was in the middle of a full-scale dispute. We were all jittery, and now it was coming out in this ridiculous brouhaha about whether or not we were too close. By now the little Fiat was rocking and I said, "Christ, Mr. Alterman, are you *trying* to wake Barbara up?"

"Damn it, Mordecai," said Abramson, "move the car."

And with a pout Alterman threw the car into reverse and jolted us backwards a few yards, just as Barbara emerged from the building and looked straight at the car.

"Oh Christ," I said.

I didn't know what to do, so out of desperation I pulled my blue down vest up over my head and just sat there, peeking out at my former wife.

It was a brilliant disguise, of course: just a man sitting in a car with no head. Barbara stared at the car a little longer and began to cross the street and I thought, *This is it. She's seen us.* And she would have, of course, if we hadn't moved the car, but now she looked down the street with equal interest and walked on in the other direction.

"Oh Christ, Barbara," I whispered as she strolled away. She didn't look well. She was wearing what looked to be a domestic's uniform under a frayed green jacket, and the heel of one shoe flapped slightly behind her. In the few seconds I'd glimpsed her face she'd looked weary and drawn.

Five more minutes went by and we kept watching the doorway, waiting for the kids. I removed my glasses for a moment and rubbed my eyes; I could feel my pulse pounding in the tips of my fingers.

"Look, Tom," said Abramson.

I fumbled my glasses back on and suddenly there were my children standing in the street.

They looked disheveled, comical, beautiful in the rosy light, slinging their book bags over their shoulders and setting off for school. Mag led them forward, loping along a few steps until Sara suddenly called out to them all to stop and I could hear her say something about her gym shoes. Mag turned around and led Sara back into the apartment building, digging for her keys, leaving Ben to wait on the street.

"Get down," said Abramson, but I couldn't move, couldn't take my eyes off Ben as he stood impatiently on the corner, not ten feet from the car.

"That's Ben," I said, reaching for the door handle. "That's my boy."

But Abramson grabbed my arm and said, "Not yet. Wait for the girl."

Minutes passed and I felt as if I were about to burst. Ben stood and fidgeted a while and then seemed to decide to give up on his sisters and began to walk away, heading for school.

"Okay," said Alterman. "Get the boy. I'll drop off the letter."

I shoved the letter at Alterman and rushed out of the car. "Ben!" I said. "It's me! It's Dad!" and I snatched him up in my arms.

Ben looked up at me as I quickly kissed him. "Dad!" he gasped. "What are you *doing?*"

"Come on, Ben," I said, handing him over to Abramson. "It's okay. You're coming with me."

Ben looked up with shock into Abramson's face as Mag and Sara reemerged from the apartment.

"Daddy!" Sara called out and rushed into my arms.

I squeezed her tight and over Sara's shoulder I glimpsed Mag backing away with a horrified look.

"Mag, it's all right," I called after her as she ran toward the apartment. "There's a letter for your mom," I said. "Don't be scared."

But Mag ran to the building, almost colliding with Alterman as he dashed back from the mailboxes.

I held Sara close and tumbled back into the car. Ben was obviously offended by being handed over to Abramson and now he wriggled out of his grasp and I had both of my children in my arms. I breathed them in like oxygen: Sara's tangled hair smelled sweet and Ben smelled like dust after a sudden rain.

"What are we doing, Daddy?" Ben asked as Alterman threw the car into first and we lurched forward, and looking into Ben's face I could see he was thinking, *Oh God, here we go again. I was just getting the routine down and now it's all screwed up again.*

"We're just going on a trip," I said lightly, hugging him close again, but then immediately I knew that it was no good: I couldn't lie to them. They'd been lied to enough already. They had to know the truth. They had to come out of this fog Barbara had cast over them.

"We're going home, kids," I said. "I'm taking you home."

"But-but I'm supposed to go to Aram's after school today," Ben said, and his eyes brimmed with tears.

"And I've got a spelling test tomorrow," said Sara. "We can't just go. Momma's going to get mad at us."

The car skidded out of Hadera, and I still held them close, but now I began to lose heart. *Jesus,* I thought. *What have I done? They were better off with Barbara. They shouldn't have to go through this again. I'm doing this for me. I thought it was for them, but now they're in terrible pain and it's my goddamn fault.*

But as I held them I had this extraordinary feeling of closure, of completion. *This will pass,* I told myself, gripping them closer. *They can't digest this right away. They need a little time.*

We reached Susan and the Peugeot and all piled into it together. Sara tumbled into Susan's arms and we sat entangled in the back seat as the Peugeot cleared Hadera and bumped out onto a narrow country road.

Within twenty minutes they were calm again, almost pensive, and at one point Ben wiped the tears off his dusty cheek and said, "You know, Dad, I'm glad you're here, because it hasn't been that good."

Sara asked about Aunt Jane.

"Do you know about Uncle Henry?" I asked.

"Yes, Daddy. It's so sad," said Ben. "Grandma Kitty told us."

So, I said to myself, nodding to Susan, *Kitty* had *known where the children were.*

Ben asked how Uncle Henry had died and I told him it was a heart attack.

"I loved Uncle Henry," Sara said sadly. "He was so great. Like W. C. Fields."

They still looked radiant to me, of course, but I could see that they hadn't been thriving. They were a little green around the gills, with dark circles under their eyes, as though they'd been sick or hadn't been eating and sleeping enough, as if they'd somehow been languishing in Hadera.

The kids switched around spontaneously. Ben snuggled against Susan and Sara curled up on my lap, and all my doubts receded as the Peugeot lurched past a military outpost and onto the West Bank.

But now we were entering the most dangerous stage of the operation. We had to assume that Mag had run to get Barbara and Barbara had alerted the police. Our deadline at Rafah was noon, when the Egyptians were scheduled to close the border for the day, which meant we should have had four hours to get there. I suddenly thought of the Egyptian embassy back in Tel Aviv. Who was to say that the Egyptians wouldn't be as capricious about opening and closing the border as they'd been about the visa office? What if they opened and closed it whenever they felt like it?

The West Bank grew scruffier as we headed south, with the flatulent old Peugeot groaning and smoking in the rising heat. We passed through several Arab villages, with frayed camels mincing along the roadside and men in checkered headdresses glaring at us as we passed. Here and there little groups of children ran alongside the car, jeering at us.

We were stopped at a checkpoint outside a little village and an Israeli sergeant peered in at us as we snacked on our boxed lunches.

"What are you doing here?" he asked Abramson.

"Taking in the sights, sergeant," said Abramson, leaning out the driver's window and handing him some documents.

"Sights?" said the sergeant, squinting at Abramson's papers. "What sights? Ah," he said, suddenly nodding. "Mr. Abramson. You may pass."

"Thank you, sergeant," Abramson said.

"But Mr. Abramson," the sergeant called after us as we sped away, "this is no place for children."

There were more checkpoints along the way, and the farther south we traveled the more ominous they became: miserable outposts bristling with spikes and barbed wire and flanked by camouflaged artillery pieces. Respectful officers with holstered pistols gave way to suspicious noncoms holding Uzis, and I clutched my children even tighter as they grudgingly waved us through.

Abramson and Alterman took turns at the wheel as we drove for three more hours through a desertscape, crossing west toward the Gaza Strip. It was hot in the car with the children in our arms, and the wind was dusty through the window. For several miles we got trapped behind a lethargic army convoy of troop trucks with jostled soldiers staring grimly at us from the back. Finally, as the trucks honked indignantly, Abramson gunned the car along the shoulder and we sped ahead of them along the straight, bleak, one-lane road.

The trucks had cost us precious time; it was eleven-thirty by the time we reached Rafah, a crummy little Arab town out of Graham Greene, with ancient, labyrinthine streets of tamped dirt and stone. We drove through the center of town, where an old man in a fez spat at the car from his booth in the marketplace.

"Where the hell is the crossing?" Abramson said as we reached a dead end cut off by a tangle of barbed wire.

"I don't know," said Alterman, backing the car to a crossroads. "I thought you knew."

"I don't know," said Abramson. "Rafah was your idea."

"Well," said Alterman, "it must be here somewhere."

"Brilliant," said Abramson. "Then ask somebody."

"Who? These Arabs? Arabs are all liars."

"The *men* are all liars," said Abramson. "Ask a woman."

"Hey!" Alterman called out, waving to an old woman sitting nearby. He said something to her in Arabic and she stood and evidently told him that we could go either right or left to get to the crossing.

So Alterman wheeled around to the left and gunned it, sending a plume of dust up behind us.

The road was set low, with high banks on either side that obscured the view, and I was thinking of Alterman's warning about Palestinian boys with stones when suddenly the road curved and we nearly ran into a guard tower.

A jeep full of Israeli soldiers screeched up to us and they all climbed out and surrounded the car.

"Who are you?" one of them asked with his gun raised. "What in hell are you doing here with children?"

I placed my arms over Ben and Sara and glared back. *They've caught us,* I said to myself. *Barbara's alarm has finally caught up with us.*

They ordered Abramson out and once again he brought forth his papers and a committee of soldiers disappeared with them for a few minutes. I looked at my watch; it was a quarter of twelve.

"Come on, come on," Alterman said through his teeth as the soldiers puzzled over Abramson's documents.

Finally one of them loped back and handed him his papers. "Follow us, sir," he said with a crisp salute. "We'll lead you to the crossing."

"Here's some Egyptian money," Abramson said, handing me an envelope as we followed in the dust of the bouncing jeep. "If you run into trouble with the Egyptians, use money. It's how they do things. And when you get to Cairo, stay off the streets. Don't go out after dark. And call me when you reach the hotel. Tell me you're all right."

"I will, Jake," I said. "I will."

So we drove in the jeep's dust along another low road and after a couple of turns we found ourselves in a little tarmac parking lot. The soldiers waved to us and returned to the guard tower as we hurried out of the car and rushed toward the gate.

The crossing consisted simply of a gate and a little stucco building. Beyond the gate was a concrete platform, from which a bus ferried visitors across a short stretch of desert to the Egyptian checkpoint.

I slung my bag over my shoulder and turned and looked at Abramson.

"I can never thank you enough," I said, embracing him.

"It was you," he said, smiling at me. "You did this. Now call me," he said, standing back and shaking a finger at me. "Let me know how you are."

"I will," I said.

There was barely time for me to stutter my thank-yous at Alterman, who smiled slightly and shrugged. And then I was tugging the kids to the gate with Susan up in front, flourishing our passports.

We could see the bus pulling up to the platform for the last ride to the Egyptian border as the guard looked at each passport in turn, checking our pictures against our faces. This was the last hurdle. If he hadn't been alerted we were free.

"All right," he said, "have a nice trip," and he raised the gate.

We rushed through and raced for the bus. As we climbed aboard we all turned around and waved at Abramson and Alterman. Alterman was grinning now as he climbed into the car, and Abramson had both his thumbs upraised.

22

THE CROSSING

So we'd made it. We were free. The little bus pulled out, and we bumped along to the Egyptian border with our visas in hand. I embraced Susan across the aisle and thanked her and told her I loved her as the other passengers stared, and the kids grimaced at each other on the seat beside me. I couldn't believe I had my family back. I had to keep touching Ben and Sara to be sure they were real.

"Boy, Dad," Ben said as I pulled him next to me, "you're going to squeeze me to *death*."

The Egyptian guard took our passports and smiled at us as we disembarked. "You come see the Sphinx?" he said. "You come see the pyramids?"

"Yes," I said. "We've come to see everything."

"Very good," said the guard, opening the passports and nodding to us.

I looked past the crossing to yet another bus with an ornate sign that said "Cairo" hanging at a tilt over the windshield.

The other passengers began to file past a second guard who was giving their passports a peremptory look and cheerfully waving them through. But now our guard was frowning and flipping back and forth among our passports as if searching for something.

"You and the woman go through," he said finally, handing me the passports. "But the children must go back."

"What?" I said.

197

"The children have no visas. They must go back."

"No, no," I said, smiling politely at him. "They don't need visas. The man at your embassy told us the children don't need visas."

The soldier shrugged. "No visas, no children. That's the law."

I tried to hand back the passports. "You don't understand, damn it," I said. "We were told at your embassy that they *don't need visas.*"

Now the guard began to back away, raising his hands. "I know my business," he said. "You don't tell me my business."

I could feel my stomach giving way again, the perspiration bursting out along my brow. This couldn't be happening. I turned and looked back the hundred yards to the Israeli checkpoint. Abramson's car was raising a little stream of dust in its wake.

The money, I thought. *Abramson said to use money.*

"Okay," I said, reaching for the envelope Abramson had handed me. "There's obviously been a mistake here. It's not our fault. It's not your fault. We've done everything in good faith."

"So?" said the guard, frowning at me now.

"As you can see, we got our visas," I said. "We'd have gotten the children their visas if we'd been told to. But we'll just fill out an application now. See?" I said, "I'll pay you the fee, and we'll be on our merry way. All right? You understand?" I said, advancing on him with the envelope.

The guard grimly shook his head. "No visas, no children," he grumbled, pointing back toward Israel.

"What the hell do you want?" I said, waving the envelope at him. "We can't go back. You can't send us back. Our ride is gone."

"You go back and get the visas. Come back Monday," the guard said. By now I had drawn the attention of his buddies, who stood by with machine guns hanging from their shoulders, smoking cigarettes.

"But I can't go back. Look," I said. "I'm not an Israeli. I'm an American. Our two countries are supposed to be friends."

"What is *that* supposed to mean?" he hissed back at me, patting his holster.

Now I was dying. Everything was coming apart again.

"Let me see your supervisor," I heard myself say.

"No," he said. "It won't do any good. Children must have visas. That is the *law*," he thundered.

"I don't care anymore," I said. And it was true; I didn't. "You can't treat us this way. I demand to see your supervisor."

The guard glared at me a moment longer, and I could see Susan drawing the kids closer to her. He took our passports out of my hand and snapped his fingers, and suddenly two soldiers with machine guns were leading me away.

"It's going to be all right, kids," I said as jauntily as I could manage with the soldiers rushing me forward. "It's just a misunderstanding."

They led me into a little building with a tin roof and took me into the presence of a suave Egyptian officer sitting at a desk in an office shuttered from the sun.

He was dressed in what looked to be a naval uniform, complete with brass buttons and braid, and he gazed at me evenly as the guard briefly filled him in. He gave the guard a curt nod and ordered the two soldiers who were flanking me to stand back by the door.

"Mr. Osborne," he said in a baritone as mellifluous as Anwar Sadat's, "this is most unfortunate. That you should come all this way only to find that your children lack the necessary visas!"

"But the man at the embassy—"

"—was mistaken. A natural mistake," he said, leaning back comfortably and flicking something off the breast of his uniform. "You see, had your children been included on your own passports no visa would be required. But when they're on separate passports I'm afraid . . ."

"But why can't *you* issue us visas?"

"You see," the officer said cheerfully, raising a hand, "the crossing at Rafah is a very special checkpoint, Mr. Osborne, established at Camp David. So there are very special limitations written not only into Egyptian law but into the treaty itself, and one of those limitations is that we are expressly forbidden to issue visas."

I was devastated. He was like an officious apparition from the past.

"But we can't go back," I said. "Our transportation is gone. I've brought my children to see your beautiful country."

"I'm so sorry," he said, "but there is absolutely nothing I can do."

"Look," I said, and I could hear my voice breaking, "we're nice people. I'm an academic. I'm a teacher of history. I've come here for the holidays. I—"

I blathered on like that, blindly trying to press the right button. After a while the officer grew impatient and began to flip angrily through our passports.

"This woman you are with isn't the children's mother," he said sharply, glowering at me.

"No," I said, staring down at the floor.

"Where is she then?" he demanded. "Where is their mother?"

"She isn't with us anymore."

"Isn't with you? What do you mean? Why do *you* have the children?"

"They're my children," I said. "I take care of them. That's just the way it is."

"Then who is this *other* woman?"

At first I thought I was merely offending his Moslem sense of propriety, but then it dawned on me where his line of questioning might have been leading. Maybe he knew or at least suspected what I was up to. Maybe Barbara's alarm had somehow leapfrogged the Israelis and reached the Egyptians.

"She's—she's their governess," I said. "When I take a business trip with the children it's very difficult, so I have to bring a governess along so they can see the world while they're on vacation."

I heard myself go on to repeat that I was a professor and a nice man and all the rest of it, and the officer got a faraway look in his eye.

"So what *happened* to their mother?" he asked.

"Look," I said. "It's all so long ago."

I sagged completely now, imagining myself trying to beat my way back to Tel Aviv, returning the children to Barbara, the whole expedition unraveling like a film run backwards.

"But what happened?" the officer asked, leaning toward me. "Did she leave you?"

"Yes," I said, "she left me," and tears came to my eyes.

"And she left the children?" he asked gently.

"It's over now," I said, starting to get to my feet. "It's all in the past. Look, we'll go back. I'll take the children back."

But the officer reached across his desk and touched my wrist.

"Sit, sit," he said gently. "I am going to help you, Mr. Osborne. I am a father too."

He took out a fountain pen and opened the children's visas, writing something in them in bold Arabic script and then marking them with a stamp on his desk.

Before I could comprehend what was happening, let alone thank him, I was being escorted back out into the sunshine.

"You," the guard called out to Susan. "Join your husband."

By now a circle of soldiers had gathered around Susan and the kids, and Susan led them through uncertainly.

"*Husband?*" I could hear Ben asking her. "You mean you two got *married?*"

"No, shhh," Susan said.

"But he said *husband,*" Ben said.

"Of course not," Susan said. "We would never get married without *you.*"

"It's okay," I said as they approached. "I got their visas. We can go through."

"Thank God," Susan said, letting her shoulders drop.

"You hurry now," said the guard, pointing to the bus. "Don't make the driver wait."

So we raced for the bus and climbed aboard. Susan and I stared at each other, wondering if we finally dared to hope that we'd made it. The possibility of the Israelis getting the Egyptians to cooperate in some kind of extradition seemed too remote to consider. And even if Barbara somehow caught up with us in Egypt, what was she going to do? We had the court decree. We had the passports for the kids. I was their legal custodial father and nobody was going to mess with us.

"We're free this time," I told Susan. "We're finally free and clear."

As I watched Ben and Sara gazing out the window at the passing desert I felt reborn, as if a huge weight had been lifted off my chest. We traveled through this extraordinary landscape straight out of *Lawrence of Arabia,* all the way down to a huge metal object floating over the dunes that turned out to be the stack of a freighter passing through the Suez Canal.

We fell in with some Egyptian students on the bus who spoke English and told us where to get off for the Cairo Hilton. So we got off by the highway on what seemed to be the outskirts of Cairo and realized too late that the student must have misunderstood us or played a nasty trick, for we found ourselves in the middle of nowhere, with a crowd of Egyptians gathering around and gawking.

We stood there for hours, trying to flag down a cab, and as it grew dark some of the men in the crowd began to look at Susan and the kids like they were hot fudge sundaes. Abramson had told us to stay off the streets and out of the dark and now here we were, filthy and scared and stranded beside Cairo's answer to the Cross Bronx Expressway.

It was as if I had come to imagine that as soon as I had my kids we would all be out of danger, but now I had to realize that there was really no such thing as a crossing, no such thing as free and clear.

I began to pace up and down the curb and shout at the grinning Egyptians standing around us, and when Susan tried to calm me down, to remind me that this was the land of *insh' allah*—God's will—I snapped at her for maybe the first time since I'd met her.

Ben is a worrier, just like me, and pretty soon he was losing control as well.

"But what if we *can't* get a taxi?" he wanted to know. "What if we *never* get out of here?"

Finally, around six, a little rattletrap taxi pulled up, and the driver, seeing an opportunity, shooed some poor Egyptian out and beckoned us in.

"Where take you please? Where take you please?" he asked as we hurried in and closed the door after us. A dozen children began to bang their arms and legs against the car.

"The Hilton," I said, guessing that there might be one in Cairo. The driver pulled away and within five minutes we found ourselves in the midst of palm trees and lawns and doormen and bellboys. I paid off the cabby and we walked to the reception desk like a family of foul and dusty tramps. The room clerk curled his lip at the sight of us and told us there were no vacancies, but I knew enough by now to prevail upon the manager. After a few minutes of palaver we floated up to our room, where there was plumbing and towels and an ice box and champagne and beer and sandwiches: and there were the kids, my kids, standing on the balcony and gazing across the distant Nile.

It was Christmas Eve and all the flights home were booked, so I made reservations for a flight to Boston early the next morning. I called Abramson as I'd promised and thanked him again for everything.

"You know," he had to confess to me, "I was a little dubious about this operation until I listened to you talking with your children in the car this morning. Then I knew that what we were doing was right."

I called Sid next and caught him on his way into his firm's Christmas party. When I broke the news I could hear a cheer go up behind him.

"I've been worrying about you all week," Sid said. "I don't like to lose control of these things, you know."

"Well, it worked, Sid. Our plan worked."

"*Mazal tov,* Tom," Sid said over the din. "We'll drink our first toast to your success."

We toured around a little the following day and caught our plane early Christmas morning. We were still pretty beat. Ben was airsick on the flight back and had to come off the plane in a wheelchair.

I was a little concerned that somehow there might be a question about the kids' passports in Boston, but they let us through without a hitch, and since we had only the one suitcase, customs was a breeze.

I left Susan and the kids to wait in the lounge and ran off to long-term parking to fetch the car. There had been a terrible freeze since we'd left, and when I got to the car it wouldn't start.

I ran back to the terminal and said, "The hell with it, Susan. We're taking a cab to Aunt Jane's." After a strange ride through the deserted yuletide streets of Boston, we arrived to find the Osborne clan sitting down to Christmas dinner.

The family had been united by the twin tragedies of Uncle Henry's death and the children's abduction, so when the front door opened, and we walked in like shivering apparitions from some Dickensian pageant, there was rejoicing. We all sang carols together that night, just as Uncle Henry had promised. The children opened their presents, and in the dappled light of the family tree their faces seemed to bloom with color.

We had a second Christmas of our own back in Alden the next morning, and after all our gifts had been unwrapped under Susan's silver tree, I led Ben and Sara out to the boathouse and unveiled their orphaned craft. "What'll we call it?" asked Ben, running his hand along its hull.

"I know," Sara said. "Let's call it the *Egypt*."

23

GRACE

In the end Barbara and her Israeli lawyer fell for my ploy and never did sound an alarm. When Abramson called to report that I had taken the children back to the States, her lawyer exclaimed, "But that can't be. Barbara's got their passports."

Barbara didn't contact the children for over a month, and when she finally did call all she had to say to me was, "How can you be so cruel?"

I wasn't inclined to resuscitate Barbara's motherhood again, and Susan was not eager to draw Barbara back into our lives, but I knew that for Ben and Sara's sake I was going to have to arrange a means by which Barbara could safely visit with the children.

I insisted on some supervision, however: there had to be a social worker or a police officer in attendance to prevent her from abducting Ben and Sara again. But Barbara couldn't seem to make the arrangements at her end.

I called Yantorno's office to ask the county to lift the felony warrant temporarily in order to facilitate her visiting the children in Alden. But Yantorno had since left the D.A.'s office, and I was transferred to his successor.

"I can't do it, Mr. Osborne," he told me. "We intend to prosecute her to the full extent of the law. She violated the laws of the commonwealth."

"Look," I told him. "The commonwealth didn't do us any good when I was trying to get my children back. I don't see how it's going to do us any good sending their mother to Framingham State Prison."

"Mr. Osborne," he replied, "I don't think you fully realize what a terrible thing she did."

One night a few months later, Ben came to Susan with another of his anguished confessions. He'd been thinking, he said, and he just couldn't keep it from us any longer. He wanted us to know that the abduction had really been his fault, because at some point during his sojourn at the Dunrollin Motel he'd turned to Barbara and said, "Mom, you've got to get us out of this."

Anyone who understands Ben knows that he's a boy who thinks that change is bad. Ben didn't think he wanted a new mother because he didn't know what it was going to be like, and for Ben not knowing has always been excruciating.

Susan tried to assure Ben that he couldn't have triggered the abduction, offering Barbara's prior attempt in August as proof. But I'm afraid that both Ben and Sara are still struggling with an implacable sense of complicity.

I guess I'll never know Barbara's end of the story: her gambles and intentions, her feints and ploys. All I know is what I've been able to surmise from the dribs and drabs the kids let slip in passing. But it seems that on the morning of the abduction, Barbara led Ben and Sara into a taxi and told them that they were going to pick up a friend of hers in Boston. They couldn't understand why Barbara was taking their suitcases along, but they figured maybe they were going to stay in town overnight. It wasn't until they reached the airport that Barbara gathered them around her and told them that they were going to visit Israel together for a while.

But what about Daddy? Sara wanted to know.

Barbara assured them that I knew all about it and that I believed it was for the best because I wanted to be alone with my new girlfriend.

The kids bought this lie until Barbara called her parents and Ben spoke to his grandfather Stanley. During the course of the conversation, Ben tried to assure Stanley that everything was fine: I'd okayed the whole thing because I wanted to be with Susan.

"But Ben," Stanley told him, "don't you understand what your mother has *done?*"

By taking the children to Hadera, Barbara had seemed to confirm my theory that the abduction was just a gesture: that once the thrill was gone she would want me to take the children off her hands.

But now I'm not so sure. Barbara may have genuinely believed that Hadera was the last place I would have looked.

Once they'd all settled in Hadera, Ben and Sara evidently became attached to the school social worker who specialized in acclimatizing immigrant children. But I don't know very much about their time in school. The other day Sara was getting frustrated with her math homework and said, "Well, what do you expect? All the math I ever got was from a lady speaking some weird language."

I've tried not to press Ben and Sara for more details about their life in Hadera, but the one person I couldn't resist asking about directly was Marcus Fleischer.

It had been my theory all along that Barbara wouldn't have done anything to risk her settlement money unless she thought she had someone else to turn to, and I figured that someone had to be Marcus.

But at first Sara couldn't figure out who I was talking about.

"You know. *Marcus*," I said. "Mommy's friend."

"Oh, *him*," she said. "He left *early*. Marcus is such a brat, Daddy. He's so *immature*."

I could hear Barbara's voice in that; Sara must have heard her mother seething out loud about him.

I still can't be sure what Barbara had meant about Marcus's coming to the birthday party: whether he'd actually been in the vicinity, facilitating things, or whether Barbara meant that he'd come to some birthday party she'd planned for the children back in Israel. But Marcus did hang around them when they reached Israel and helped Barbara enroll the kids in school, leaving instructions with the staff to notify him if anyone made inquiries about them.

Marcus didn't hang around for long, and my current guess is that he was probably just a rich kid who'd thought he'd landed a nice American mistress but suddenly found himself looking after a felon with a bunch of kids.

After Marcus fell away, Barbara began to run out of money fast. She tried to make a living as a sidewalk portrait artist and a domestic, but, like everything else in Israel, her apartment was expensive, and

Barbara fell behind in her rent. By December the gas had been turned off and the phone removed, and they'd begun to run out of food.

Her situation became so desperate that sometime in the late fall she evidently called her lawyer to see if he could get more money out of me. But by this point he had had his fill of Barbara and told her to forget it; there was a felony warrant out for her arrest in Massachusetts, and the FBI was on her trail.

After Kitty informed Barbara that I was running some kind of school computer search, Barbara evidently took to leading the kids in a little suppertime grace that ended with, "And please, God, don't let Daddy find us."

To which Ben would add, "But I really hope he does," whispering it into his napkin.

When the kids got home and the houses along the cove emptied out after the holidays, we watched Ben and Sara like hawks. We deposited not only a court order but a whole legal brief with Principal Lepke, and one of us always escorted Ben and Sara to the school bus in the morning and met them in the afternoon. When Barbara didn't call those first weeks I worried that she might try to take my kids again and disappear with them for good. Andy Flynn promised to keep an eye out for suspicious cars along the point.

Even after Barbara and I were back in touch, the level of communication was so poisonous at first that it took me months to trust that the felony warrant would keep her at bay. It wasn't until I realized that the kids themselves were older and wiser and much less likely victims that I finally backed off a little.

No matter how well things may turn out after an abduction, some things remain broken forever. The kidnapping will haunt my children and me for the rest of our lives. I've had to tell myself that this is just the way it is, that some of the trust and security and certitude of the past can never be recovered, and all we can do is build on what's left.

But as I watched Susan gently draw Ben and Sara toward her, trusting them when they could not trust themselves, seeing them through their rage and confusion, and coaxing them back onto solid ground, I wished all of us could be born with her strength and security and capacity to abide.

As I make it to the surface and put my life together again, I'm sorry that Barbara didn't have all of that going for her, that the earth wasn't more comfortable for her. I can see now that her marginality wasn't a weapon directed at me, but an impairment. The kids and I were free, but she was still caught in the maelstrom.*

So much of my life has fallen back into place that it seems almost symphonic. But if there's still a dissonance in the final cadences, it is my daughter Mag. She remains the innocent victim of my collision with Barbara, and I can never forget her horrified stare as I gathered up Ben and Sara. There are no tidy solutions to the mess Barbara and I made of our life together, but I hope that I can someday draw Mag back to the family.

Some afternoons when it's getting dark and Ben and Sara are a little late returning from a playmate's house, I still can't keep from hurrying off to find them. If I can't spot them from the road or if I've somehow crossed signals with another parent, panic takes over, and soon I'm calling the police and racing up and down the point, peering into yards and ringing doorbells and sounding a general alarm. And then I'll catch sight of Ben shambling along the shore or I'll hear Sara singing to herself as she skips up the walk, and I'll scoop them up like butterflies and carry them indoors.

As I begin to fall off to sleep some nights, I find I'm visited by a mutation of the widow Folkes: a disheveled woman in an old car with a battered grill cruises my nightmares now, slowing as she nears my children and opening her door.

So I rise from my bed, and I go again to Ben and Sara and draw their blankets up around them and reassure myself of the sweetness of existence with the steady music of their breathing.

EPILOGUE

The Orthodox rabbis who adjudicate applications under the Law of Return repudiated Barbara Kaye Osborne's conversion and refused to grant her Israeli citizenship. Deported as an indigent in March of 1984, she moved with Mag to Canada, where she now lives.

The felony warrant in Massachusetts is still pending. Barbara did arrange a supervised visit with Ben and Sara in Montreal in 1986, and thus saw her children for the first time in three years. Their visits are continuing.

After Barbara and Mag were settled in Canada, Osborne began to send regular monthly payments of $200 in child support for Mag. As of this writing Mag has resumed regular contact with Osborne and has visited her brother and sister in Alden.

Stanley Thorpe was promoted to a senior position in the Justice Department in Washington. Rick Yantorno left the D.A.'s office for private practice. Peter Hill left the firm of Partridge, Osborne and Lanier, whose bill for $3,500 Osborne refused to pay in full.

Osborne paid Sidney Kugler $10,000 and remains his client. Mordecai Alterman, the Israeli detective, charged $3,500. Jacob Abramson paid Osborne's hotel bill in Tel Aviv and charged him $2,500, including expenses.

Thomas Osborne and Susan Peale were married in June of 1984. Osborne is now a professor of history at a college in Boston, and Susan has resumed her ceramics business in Alden.

Almost three years after recovering Ben and Sara, Osborne built a house for his family on a wooded lot in the Peaceable Kingdom that Uncle Henry had left to him. As I walked with Tom along Osborne Point in the early fall of 1986, he saw for the first time the lights of his new home shining through the woods across the cove.

NOTES

Page 111
Attorney Geva's letter is reproduced verbatim and uncorrected.

Page 118
Walsh is a composite of the two assistant U.S. attorneys who concerned themselves with Osborne's case, both of whom declined to be interviewed for this book.

Page 128
The UFAP process has come under attack by civil liberties lawyers, who regard it as a violation of a fugitive's right to due process, and for that reason, and because its actual purpose is served as soon as the fugitive is turned over, no U.S. Attorney has ever prosecuted a UFAP violation. The U.S. Attorney's office therefore requires less evidence for a UFAP warrant than it would if it were contemplating an actual prosecution in court.

Page 130
From October 1, 1983, to September 30, 1984, the FBI reported 1,448 parental kidnapping cases received, 1,206 resolved, and 297 pending. During the next twelve months it reported 1,383 received, 1,273 resolved, and 407 pending.

By "resolved" the FBI does not mean solved but merely the number of cases on which the FBI has made a determination. "Resolved" therefore includes not only those few cases in which request for a UFAP application has been granted, the abducting parent has been arrested, and the children returned to their custodial parent, but also, and predominantly, those cases in which applications were denied. Thus, by the FBI's definition, Osborne's was one of the 1,448 cases it had resolved. When the FBI was asked how many of these cases had ended in the return of abducted children, it replied that no such figures were kept.

Page 131

The criminalization of parental abduction has provided some parents and D.A.'s with the leverage with which to recover children, but it has yet to serve as a deterrent, primarily because once children are recovered, D.A.'s are loath to prosecute abducting parents. For D.A.'s no less than for U.S. Attorneys, parental abduction cases are unappetizing. It disturbs many prosecutors that the merits of a criminal proceeding in a parental abduction case will be determined by the civil proceeding that decided custody in the first place, in which judicial discretion and evidentiary parameters are much broader.

In addition, the prospect of cross-examining a distraught mother who has abducted her children does not exactly cause ambitious young prosecutors' hearts to leap, nor do they rejoice at the prospect of arguing before a jury that it's somehow in the best interest of a mother's children to throw her in jail.

Most proponents of criminalization concede that incarceration is not necessarily a remedy for individual families already traumatized by an abduction; on the other hand they firmly believe that the law won't deter abductions if prosecutors refuse to prosecute, juries refuse to convict, and judges refuse to incarcerate parental abductors.

Despite changes in state statutes and Justice Department regulations favoring custodial parents during the past three years, noncustodial parents who abduct their children continue to run an almost negligible risk of arrest or prosecution.

Page 209

On October 16, 1987, the State Department agreed to establish a bureau to handle inquiries from Americans whose children have been abducted overseas. According to Senator Alan J. Dixon, Democrat from Illinois, who is seeking to make international abduction a federal offense, there has been an 80 percent rise in the number of such abductions since 1983. Only 4 percent of the children in the 2,543 cases reported to the State Department have been recovered.

From Children's Rights of Pennsylvania, Inc.:

Many ex-spouses signal their intention to abduct children. Being aware of the following signs may enable you to protect your children against this crime.

1. *A negative reaction to your plans to remarry, relocate, or in any other way alter your lifestyle.*
2. *An abrupt change in an ex-spouse's attitude toward you or the children, such as a spirit of cooperation where there had been hostility, or the opposite.*
3. *Signs of unstable behavior.*
4. *Changes in your ex-spouse's lifestyle, such as remarriage, a new job, or plans to relocate.*
5. *A request to take the children for a longer period of time than usual.*

What to do if you fear a parental abduction:

1. *If you are separated, obtain legal custody.*
2. *If litigation is in process, you may need consent of the court prior to leaving its jurisdiction. Explain, preferably through your lawyer, that you think there is a real danger of abduction and you want to protect your child's right to see you.*
3. *Specify visitation rights as precisely as possible in divorce or custody papers. Know where your child will be taken on visitations, address and phone number of ex-spouse, and license plate number of the car in which your child leaves for a visit.*
4. *Bonds of numerous types are available to help ensure the return of child. You and your lawyer may need to convince the court of the need for one.*
5. *It's sometimes possible to obtain a court order allowing visitation only under supervision if you can convince the court there is a threat of abduction.*
6. *If children are of school age, include in the custody order a provision to prohibit the transfer of school papers without prior approval of the custodial parent. File this with the school.*

To which I would add:

7. *File a court order with the passport office and request that no passport be granted for your children without your notification and approval.*

Additional guidance, especially regarding how to instruct your children about abduction, is available from:

> National Center for Missing & Exploited Children
> 1835 K Street, N.W., Suite 700
> Washington, D.C. 20006

ACKNOWLEDGMENTS

There are many participants in this story who graciously granted me interviews and extended many kindnesses, but whose names I cannot reveal because of the need to protect the Osbornes' privacy. I hope that their own knowledge of their assistance to Tom and his family will compensate for their anonymity on these pages.

I want to thank the staffs of the many groups that concern themselves with the issue of parental abduction for their contributions to my understanding of this baffling problem. Parental abduction is complex and vulnerable to many conflicting agendas. My acknowledgment of assistance from the following people should not be construed as implying that they agree with or approve of Mr. Osborne's actions or my own conclusions about parental abduction. These people are: Judy Cochran and Phyllis Watts of Children's Rights of Pennsylvania; June Vlasaty, Executive Director of Child Care, the Society for Young Victims; Carolyn Zogg (Associate Director) and Nat Baker (Investigator) of Child Find Incorporated; Kathy Rosenthal, Executive Director of Children's Rights of America, Incorporated; Betty DiNova, Founding Director of the Dee Scofield Awareness Program, Incorporated; Jan Russell, Executive Director of the Illinois Task Force on Parental Child Abduction; Dennis D. Williams, Chief Executive Officer of Kidwatch, Incorporated; Cathy Knapp, President of Mothers Without Custody (MW/OC); Charles Pickett, Technical Advisor to the National Center for Missing and Exploited Children; Joe Anneken, Director of the Office of International Missing Children Search of the National Child Safety Council; Charles A. Sutherland, Trustee of Search Reports Incorporated; Georgia Hilgeman, Executive Director of Vanished Children's Alliance; Gary Rosenfeldt, President of Victims of Violence (Canada).

Those who want to know more about the problem of parental abduction should contact the National Center for Missing & Exploited Children at 1835 K Street, N.W., Suite 700, Washington, D.C. 20006. The Center maintains an updated list of local organizations that concern themselves with this problem, and publishes some of the most definitive publications on the subject. For those who have information that could lead to the location and recovery of a missing child, the Center asks that you call their toll-free hotline at 800/843-5678.

I want to thank William Carter, Public Affairs Specialist for the Office of Congressional and Public Affairs at the Federal Bureau of Investigation, and Peter H. Pfund, Assistant Legal Advisor to the State Department, for contributing to my understanding of the federal government's approach to parental abduction.

I also want to thank former assistant U.S. Attorney Hugh W. Cuthbertson, as well as other assistant U.S. attorneys who provided their perspective on federal UFAP procedures in cases of parental abduction, but who wish to remain anonymous. Assistant District Attorney Joseph Green for Essex County, Massachusetts, was especially helpful to me in providing clippings and legal references pertaining to parental abduction and in demonstrating the efficacy of pursuing abductors in criminal court.

Thanks also to Debbie for her wisdom and Jake and Casey for their patience as I wrestled with Tom's story. I wish to thank my godfather, Professor Emeritus Andrew Bongiorno of Oberlin College, for continuing my education by correcting the manuscript without scolding its author. I am also indebted to Jeremy Nussbaum and John Hawkins for helping me navigate the shoals of nonfiction and to my editor, Kathryn Court, for her enthusiasm for this project and for her characteristically careful and sensitive reading.

I regret that I was not able to include the stories of the mothers and fathers who contacted me about their children's abductions as I researched this book. I hope these pages are informed by their anguish and their faith.

SOURCES

This book is based primarily on extensive interviews with the participants in this story and the documentation kindly provided me by Tom and Susan, especially the notes Susan kept during their search for Ben and Sara. In examining the legal context and implications of Tom's story, I found the following material useful. I hope that parents who find themselves in circumstances similar to Tom's may benefit from them.

Books

Abrahms, Sally. *Children in the Crossfire: The Tragedy of Parental Kidnapping.* New York: Atheneum, 1984.

Agopian, Michael W. *Parental Child-Stealing.* Lexington, Mass.: D.C. Heath & Co., 1981.

Black, Bonnie Lee. *Somewhere Child.* New York: Viking, 1981.

Bodenheimer, Brigitte. *Progress Under the Uniform Child Custody Jurisdiction Act and Remaining Problems: Punitive Decrees, Joint Custody and Excessive Modifications.* California Law Review 65 (1977).

The Child Custody Project, Patricia M. Hoff, Esq., Director. *Interstate and International Child Custody Disputes: A Monograph.* American Bar Association Fund for Public Education, Washington, D.C., 1982.

Clinkscales, John Dixon. *Kyle's Story: Friday Never Came.* New York: Vantage Press, 1981.

Demeter, Anna. *Legal Kidnapping.* Boston: Beacon Press, 1977.

Fielding, Joy. *Kiss Mommy Goodbye*. New York: Doubleday & Co., 1981.

Gill, John Edward. *Stolen Children*. New York: Seaview Books, 1981.

Hoff, Patricia, Joanne Schulman, and Adrienne Volenik. *Interstate Child Custody Disputes and Parental Kidnapping: Policy, Practice and Law*, American Bar Association, Legal Services Corporation, 1982.

Katz, Sanford N. *Child Snatching: The Legal Response to the Abduction of Children*. Chicago: American Bar Association Press, 1981.

National Association for Missing Children. *My Child Is Not Missing*. Child Safe Products, Inc., Florida, 1984.

National Center for Missing and Exploited Children. *Child Protection*. Washington, D.C., undated.

———. *Directory of Support Systems and Resources for Missing and Exploited Children*. Washington, D.C., undated.

———. *Investigator's Guide to Missing Child Cases*. Washington, D.C., undated.

———. *Parental Kidnapping*. Washington, D.C., undated.

———. *Selected State Legislation*. Washington, D.C., undated. *The N.C.M.E.C.'s continuously updated materials on missing and exploited children are the most authoritative available.*

Office of Citizen Consular Services, United States Department of State. *Locating a Missing Child Abroad*. Washington, D.C., 1983.

Olsen, Jack. *Have You Seen My Son?* New York: Atheneum, 1982.

Ramos, Suzanne. *The Complete Book of Child Custody*. New York: G. P. Putnam's Sons, 1979.

Roman, Mel, and William Haddad. *The Disposable Parent*. New York: Holt, Rinehart & Winston, 1978.

Silver, Gerald A. and Myrna. *Weekend Fathers*. Los Angeles: Stratford Press, 1981.

Strickland, Margaret. *How to Deal with Parental Kidnapping*. Rainbow Books, 1983.

———. *Parental Kidnapping: An International Resource Directory*. Rainbow Books, 1986.

Related Materials

Anderson, Paul. "3.3m OK'd to find missing children." *The Boston Globe*, 19 April 1984.

Armerding, Taylor. "Parental kidnapping a holiday problem." *Salem News*, 27 December 1982.

———. "Child kidnapping: Act of revenge by bitter parents." *Salem News*, 28 December 1982.

———. "Holland vs. Holland—A custody fight." *Salem News*, 29 December 1982.

Burke, Kevin M., and Frederick E. Berry. "An Act Relative to the Crime of Abduction of Children by Relatives." Petition accompanied by bill, Senate No. 163. Commonwealth of Massachusetts, 1986.

Collins, Henry. "Burke vows to stop kidnappers." *Salem News*, 2 October 1985.

Coombs, Russell M. "Curbing the Child Snatching Epidemic." *Family Advocate*, vol. 6, no. 4 (Spring, 1984).

Driscoll, Anne. "New law untangles child-snatching cases." *Salem News*, undated.

Foley, Christopher, and Patricia Hoff. "Prosecutors, Police and Parental Kidnapping." *The Prosecutor* (Summer, 1982).

Green, Joseph B. Essex County, Massachusetts Assistant District Attorney. "Child Snatching." Memo, 4 March 1981.

———. "Speaking Out. Parental Kidnapping: Massachusetts Law and Police Responsibility." *Essex County Criminal Justice Report*, vol. 1, no. 3 (May-June, 1985).

———. "The Crime of Parental Kidnapping in Massachusetts." *Massachusetts Law Review* (Fall, 1985).

———. "Parental Kidnapping: Essex County Statistics 1983–85." 1986.

———. "An Act Relative to the Crime of Abduction of Children by Relatives: Rationale for Changing G.L., h.265, §26A." Undated.

———. "Notes for Kidnapping Talk." Undated.

Heaney, Joe. "A son 'held hostage.' " *The Boston Herald*, 21 August 1985.

McLaughlin, Jim. "Getting away with kidnapping." *Sunday Eagle-Tribune* (Lawrence, Massachusetts), 15 June 1983.

National Organization for Victim Assistance (NOVA) Newsletter. "Missing Children's Act." September, 1982.

Newsweek. "Stolen Children." 19 March 1984.

O'Connell, Steve. "Kidnapping by parents targeted by D.A." *Beverly Times*, 16 June 1986.

Orrigan, Ernest J. "Parents account for most kidnappings." Ottaway News Service. *Gloucester Times*, 19 February 1985.

Salem News. "Bill makes 'child snatching' a felony." 14 June 1983.

Smith, Greg B. "When parents are the kidnappers." *The Boston Globe,* undated.

Wish, Dr. Peter A. "Messy divorce extends to child stealing." *The Haverhill, Massachusetts Gazette,* 16 November 1983.